*You think people wouldn't like it if they found out that every-
thing was done by deals?*

I don't think so; I don't think most people would like it, cause
that's making the American way of life sort of, like, the justice,
the freedom, you can pull yourself up, the Abraham Lincoln
thing, where you can come from a log cabin to the president, the
White House, you know . . . they fucked all that up, you know.

A DEFENDANT, 1971

JONATHAN D. CASPER

is a member of the Department of Political Science at Stanford University.

Professor Casper is also the author of two other recent books on the American legal system: Lawyers Before the Warren Court *and* The Politics of Civil Liberties.

American Criminal Justice

Justice

the defendant's perspective

JONATHAN D. CASPER

A SPECTRUM BOOK

PRENTICE-HALL, INC., ENGLEWOOD CLIFFS, N.J.

Library of Congress Cataloging in Publication Data

CASPER, JONATHAN D
American criminal justice.

(A Spectrum Book)
1. Criminal justice, Administration of—United States. I. Title.
KF9223.Z9C35   345'.73'05   72–4484
ISBN 0–13–024034–6
ISBN 0–13–024026–5 (pbk.)

10 9 8 7 6 5 4 3

Prentice-Hall International, Inc. (*London*)
Prentice-Hall of Australia, Pty. Ltd. (*Sydney*)
Prentice-Hall of Canada, Ltd. (*Toronto*)
Prentice-Hall of India Private Limited (*New Delhi*)
Prentice-Hall of Japan, Inc. (*Tokyo*)

To Mary

R. Smith

CONTENTS

ix

PREFACE

This is one more in a growing group of books dealing with the administration of criminal justice in America, but it differs from many in its perspective. Rather than examine the process from the perspective of a judge, prosecutor, defense lawyer, or neutral observer, I examine the administration of justice from the perspective of the defendant—perhaps the most important "consumer" of criminal justice. His is by no means the only useful viewpoint, but it is one that should not be ignored, as it largely has been until recently. It is the defendant who must most directly live with the consequences of the administration of criminal justice; moreover, given the current concern with crime, it is the defendant's past and future behavior that is of concern not only to him but also to our society at large. Thus, to examine what the defendant thinks is happening to him, the roots of his behavior, and the lessons he learns from his encounter with criminal justice is of importance in understanding the operation and impact of one set of institutions of American government.

In large measure, then, this book is descriptive, detailing the defendants' views of the individuals and institutions of criminal justice. I also offer some interpretations of the defendants' perceptions and attitudes, attempting to suggest their source and implications. I have attempted to place the analysis in the background, for the major purpose of this work is to permit defendants to speak for themselves, to have a voice in describing a process with which they are so vitally concerned.

Because of the limited number of defendants interviewed, the material presented here must be evaluated with care. Seventy-one defendants were interviewed for periods averaging about an hour and a half. All the men interviewed had been charged with felonies in Connecticut. Forty-nine of the men were incarcerated in Connecticut correctional institutions; of the remaining twenty-two, sixteen were on probation, and six had received dismissals or acquittals. The men in prison were selected randomly; the men on the street were a self-selected sample: letters to men selected randomly from various court records and newspaper reports were sent out, and about one-half of those contacted agreed to be interviewed. The interviews of all men were tape recorded and transcribed verbatim. The quotations in the text are from the transcripts, sometimes edited for continuity.

Thus, the sample of men—all of whom come from a single jurisdiction—is limited in number and consists predominantly of those who were ultimately convicted. Generalizing from this group to all of American criminal justice is a risky enterprise and one that I have attempted to avoid. But I think that the patterns in attitudes discussed here may have relevance to defendants throughout much of America. The strength of such exploratory research is its ability to challenge common wisdom and suggest questions for further research. Thus, many reservations about the findings presented here may in fact be questions for further research.

The book has one other purpose. Almost everyone who has contact with American criminal justice is led to the conclusion that it is in rotten shape; certainly that is my conclusion and one of the points argued here. Clearly there are a variety of reasons for the difficulties in changing the institutions of criminal justice: disagreements about what ought to be done, problems in resource allocation, disagreements about where the responsibility for change lies. I believe that another factor is also crucial: defendants are very much outsiders in American life, not enjoying the fruits of organized interest-group activity in their behalf and, even more basically, suffering from an image in the eyes of many people in our society as something less than complete human beings.

Much of the rhetoric dealing with criminals speaks in terms of the crazed killer or mugger or the glassy-eyed junkie. Certainly such men exist in our society, and some of the men I spoke with fit this description. But most of my respondents did not seem emotionally disturbed; nor were they less than complete human beings. They were men, though men with problems: sometimes psychological, more often social or economic. If you ask yourself whether men who commit crimes are like everyone else—some smart, some dull; some nice, some mean; some sensitive, some crude—you are likely to quickly answer, Yes, of course they are. When you go into prison and talk to criminals and find that in fact this is true, you are a bit surprised, despite your a priori protestations. This prejudice seems to me in large measure responsible for the failure of our society to deal more effectively and helpfully with those who commit deviant acts. One of the purposes of this book, then, is simply to permit some of the men to speak for themselves, to reveal that they *are* like the rest of us, that they are deserving of our attention and concern.

I owe a great number of debts for help in conducting this research. Financial assistance was provided by the National Institute of Law Enforcement and Criminal Justice of the Law Enforcement Assistance Administration, by the Social Science Research Council, and by Yale University. The Connecticut Department of Correction was kind enough to permit me to conduct interviews in two of its institutions. I am especially indebted to Frank Carpenter, Charles Dean, Carl Townsend, and Ronald Studebaker of the Correction Department for their many courtesies in arranging and providing facilities for my interviews.

I am indebted to Milton Heumann for his assistance in arranging interviews with men on the street; they were hard to locate, and his enthusiasm and charm were essential to my gaining their cooperation. The transcription of the interviews was done by Katherine Rae, Merrilyn Belliveau, Martha Brown, and Leslie Carr. Their patience and sensitivity in capturing both the substance and the flavor of the men's remarks are deeply appreciated. Mary Hankamer, Douglas Rae, and Dennis Curtis provided me with general encouragement and many useful suggestions in the analysis and presentation of the material included here. Robert Heidel of Spectrum Books contributed invaluable editorial assistance.

Finally, I am most indebted to the defendants themselves, for without their willingness to talk to me, the research simply would not have been possible.

Given the support and involvement of government institutions in this research, the disclaimer that the views expressed here are solely my own is not only traditional but required.

1

Introduction

What is it like to be arrested, go to court, be convicted, and perhaps sent to prison? The application of the criminal sanction is perhaps the most serious and destructive measure that the government can take against a citizen. The character of the administration of justice, furthermore, is a crucial indicator of the justness of the government and of the quality of life in a society regulated by law.

Images of the criminal process abound, and they offer various and often contradictory interpretations of reality in American society. On television we see a dramatic, carefully controlled process, in which each side is represented by committed, often brilliant attorneys jealously guarding and defending the rights of their clients. Mistakes may be made, but truth and justice generally triumph: the guilty are convicted and punished, and the innocent are vindicated and set free. We see the adversary process at its finest, operating to protect the rights of defendants and to arrive at a judgment conforming to absolute truth.

If, on the other hand, we listen to professional prosecutors, police officers, and other critics of recent Supreme Court decisions, a somewhat different picture emerges. We see a victimized majority and hamstrung police and prosecutors, unable to deal effectively with those who violate the law. We see a scale balanced unevenly in favor of the criminal defendant. These critics conjure up the image of the crazed bad man—the mugger, the rapist, the junkie—free to pursue his heinous activities because of procedural protections that hamper his capture, conviction, and punishment.

If, finally, we examine the growing body of reformist and scholarly literature dealing with the criminal justice system, we find the image of an assembly line. The system is a machine which begins with raw material consisting of those arrested. They are processed and emerge as a product: the convicted criminal, sentenced to prison or released on probation. Between arrest and disposition are a series of points on the assembly line: the preliminary hearing, the stay in jail awaiting trial, the bargaining about a "deal" (e.g., a reduction of charges in exchange for a guilty plea), the cop-out (plea of guilty), and sentencing day. The machine has some quality controls, and some of the objects are "rejected" and thrown off the assembly line at various stages, as charges are dropped, witnesses don't show up, imperfections in the state's case emerge. But the machine grinds on, processing its materials and turning over cases. The crucial aspects of the process—the bargaining, the quality of legal representation, the role of the defendant himself—are determined by a necessity to keep the system functioning, to ensure that it does not collapse under the weight of its own work.

Which of these divergent images is most like reality? There are a variety of avenues which might be explored in attempting to discover which is the most correct image. We could look at the process from the perspective of the judge, of the prosecutor, of the defense attorney, of a disinterested observer. All of these are important perspectives, worthy of exploration. A good deal of literature viewing the process from these perspectives is available. It is important to realize that the concept of "reality" as a kind of abstract truth about the process is chimerical. The reality of the system presumably varies from perspective to perspective. The police officer or prosecutor decrying the sacrifice of effective law enforcement in the name of individual rights can point to many concrete instances in which this in fact has occurred. The libertarian who decries the system as a machine, who argues that the defendant is but an object on an assembly line, who suggests that the outcomes of cases and the sentences imposed have more to do with the production ethic than the needs of the individual defendant can, likewise, point to a "reality" which supports this position.

Thus, to understand the process, to get a grasp on its many realities, requires a number of perspectives. This book looks at the process from a perspective that has, by and large, been ignored. This is the perspective of what I call the "consumer" of criminal justice: the defendant himself. This perspective is important not simply because it can add another dimension to our understanding of criminal justice. It is crucial because the defendant is, in many ways, the most important participant in the process: he is alleged to have committed the crime; he will have to go to jail or be set free. When the government intervenes in his life, it is, literally, his life that is involved. Hence, any evaluation of our system, any attempt to describe it or change it, must take his views and perspective into account. As Edmund Cahn suggests:

> Only when we . . . adopt a consumer perspective are we able to perceive the practical significance of our institutions, laws, and public transactions in terms of their impacts on the lives and homely experiences of human beings. It is these personal impacts that constitute the criteria for any appraisal we may make. How, we ask, does the particular institution affect personal rights and personal concerns, the interests and aspirations of the individual, group, and community? We judge it according to its concussions on human lives.[1]

In this book we examine the consumer's perspective on American criminal justice. What do defendants think is happening to them? What do they think other participants—police officers, defense attorneys, prosecutors, judges—are doing? What lessons do they learn from their encounter with the system of the administration of justice? What do the "concussions on human lives" of the criminal system tell us about effectiveness in attaining its goals of apprehension, punishment, and rehabilitation? What do they tell us about the quality of justice and life for a segment of American society?

I shall begin discussion of these questions by reproducing (with slight editing for continuity) a segment of an interview with a man currently serving an eleven-to-fifteen-year prison sentence for manslaughter. In a variety of ways he was not typical of the seventy-one men with whom I spoke. He had no prior criminal record. He was thirty-three, somewhat older than most of the men interviewed. He had a year's college education, substantially above average. A few months before his offense he held a responsible supervisory position with a large corporation and made a salary much greater than that which others had attained or could hope to attain. He was, in short, a member of the white middle class, not the group typically encountered in prison or on probation.

It is these atypical qualities that make his story interesting. He was not a street-wise man, nor was he experienced with and wise in the ways of the courts. Thus, his experience and his recounting of it are not colored by previous experience. His preconceptions of the system, like most people's, came not from experience, but from television, movies, and books. He observed and learned quickly that reality is significantly different from media images.

Here is a part of his story:

Could you tell me something about your arrest? What were you doing and what happened when the police came up?

I was walking down the street. I knew they were looking for me. I knew it was just a matter of time, really. When I saw them, I saw the cruiser across the street and I was sure that they had me and, you know, that was it.

So they stopped you. What did they say?

Well, they asked me my name, and I knew what they were lookin for and I just said, "Search me" and everything. And they told me why they were pickin me up.

What did they say you were charged with?

Murder.

Did they ask you any questions?

Not right then. They read off the rights and so forth.

How did they seem to you? Were they friendly, hostile, indifferent, matter of fact?

No, they weren't hostile. They were just doin their job, and they weren't abusive or anything. I guess when they saw how nervous I was, [they were] kind of friendly, you know.

So what happened then?

Well, I guess they were headin for the police station, but then they took me over to the apartment where it happened, to have the landlord identify me. The landlord was the one who was hostile; if they'd a let him, he'd a probably choked me to death. He was an old man; he was kind of scared, you know. It upset him pretty bad, he grabbed me, then they took me down the police station, and they started questioning me.

Now, did the landlord identify you as the guy who had done it?

No, he identified me as being the one in the apartment. It was my apartment. Well, see, he had come in, he had come up to my room and knocked on the door in the morning, and it was then that I realized I didn't have time to figure out what I was gonna do or anything. And I guess I pushed him aside and I ran. And this was probably what upset him, more or less. Well, he claimed that I hit him, and I don't really think I did. I can remember pushin him, and the witness across the hall said that I had more or less pushed him up against the wall, but it was just a matter of releasin myself. He had me around the neck.

Did the police begin to ask you questions?

Right.

Did you answer them?

Yeah, I don't know; like I say I never been in this situation before. I realized I probably shouldn't have said anything until I had seen a lawyer.

You say they did inform you of your rights?

Yeah, yeah.

And you understood them?

Yeah.

But you talked because? . . .

Well, there wasn't much point in not talkin, I guess.

You figured they had you anyway?

Yeah.

So you admitted to it?

Yeah. They had a tape recorder going, and they asked me a
few questions and I made one statement that—I couldn't sit here
right now and tell you exactly what happened. So what I said
probably wasn't any more truth than it was fiction: I mean I was
trying to come up with some kind of an answer. And I think I
made about . . . two or three recordings, different ones, you
know, statements. And this guy that questioned me, he wasn't
satisfied with any of them. He finally asked me if I would take a
lie detector test and I told him I would. But then he never did.
He just decided against it, and then finally I made a statement
he was satisfied with. He typed it out, and I signed it.

And they booked you for first-degree murder?

Right.

*Now you say they told you you had a right to a lawyer, and you
sort of considered that?*

Well, they asked me if I wanted—if I had my own lawyer, if I
wanted to call a lawyer. I told them that I did want a lawyer,
but by the time he got there, it was a public defender. Also by
the time he got there, I was in the cell and I already had made
all the statements. And he was a little upset by the fact that
I had already made a statement and so forth. He told me,
"Well," he said, "I realize the circumstances under which you
made it," he says, "so don't worry about it too much. It's rough
that you did make it, but we can probably get it taken care of,"
but I guess that that statement held up right through the whole
thing.

*Now if you can think back to the time you first encountered your
lawyer—how did you intend to plead to first-degree murder?*

Well, I don't think I would of ever pled guilty to the first-
degree murder. Because, well of course at the time, I had no
knowledge really about law. I didn't know the difference between
first degree and second degree, or what. It wasn't really until I
had gone to the grand jury that I realized just what first-degree
murder was, and it was then I knew that I wasn't guilty of first-
degree murder. Because, well, it's premeditation and what is it?
Malice, and I mean these were just completely out of the question. So, then I felt that the only thing I was guilty of would be

manslaughter, and that's the one thing I would of pleaded guilty to, which is what they finally broke it down to.

All right, let's get back to the story again. You're in jail, the lawyer shows up, says that the statement was bad but maybe they could do something about it. What happens then?

He just told me that from now on I wasn't to say a word to anybody except to him or to whoever would be assigned to me when I went to superior court.

How did this lawyer, the first lawyer, impress you?

Well, I wish he had been my lawyer all the way through.

He seemed interested in you?

Right.

Concerned? . . .

He was fairly young, and he's probably not as experienced as Mr. "Franklin," who I eventually had; but I think he would have taken more interest maybe because he would have had more time. I realize the superior court prosecut—— or the public defenders are swamped.

So what happened then? So you stay in jail?

I was there probably two or three hours, I guess. And then about eleven o'clock they brought me out, and then they took me over to "Eastport" [jail] . . . and that's when I realized how bad jail was. In [that jail] it's really bad. I guess I got there after chow, which wouldn't have made any difference anyway because as long as they take to book you in, if you get there at breakfast time, you might miss supper. No, I mean this is serious.

Yeah, I believe you.

They have three or four people working there, sentenced men working there, and their main object seems to be to get through the day without doin any work. And most of em make it, believe me. And the guards don't seem to push em. So gettin booked in really is a major ordeal. So I got lunch, which was a fish stick sandwich, and then I finally got booked in late in the afternoon. And they put me in a cell with what they call the bound-over block. They have four cells in the bottom row that are used just for dead-lock. I stayed in there for about two and a half months, I guess.

Did your lawyer visit you during this period at all?

No. Wait a minute, I'll take that back; I think the one from "Cedarville" came over there once about the first or second or third day I was there. It was more or less to tell me that I would probably be assigned to Mr. Franklin in Eastport, and, you know, just good luck and so forth.

But Franklin didn't show up during this period?

Mr. Franklin does not come to the jail. You go to him.

What was the next thing that happened to you?

I don't know what you call them, but the sheriff in Eastport came and arrested me on a bench warrant, to be bound over to superior court and then I went to court, to be bound over.

Did you talk to Franklin there?

I don't remember whether I talked to him that first day or not. Yes, I did, just very briefly, for about two or three minutes; he called me in his office.

What did he say?

He had the file there, from the other lawyer and asked me if I could tell him exactly what happened, and I told him that I didn't really remember too much of what happened. I guess he didn't seem like he wanted to go into it too much at that time; he said, "Well, we'll see what we can do," and this and that, and that was about it.

Did he say anything at that time about dropping the charge from first degree?

No, as a matter of fact, when I saw him again just before the grand jury this is one thing that surprised me in a way. I figured that with he being my defense attorney, that as soon as that grand jury was over—because he's not allowed in the hearing— that he would call me and then want to find out what went on. After that grand jury I never saw him for two months.

You stayed in jail?

Yeah.

What were you indicted for?

First degree.

First degree?

Yeah. And I mean I had sat there for a day and a half takin notes on things I thought maybe he'd want to know. And he never asked me, never saw me after the grand jury. But when I did see him about two months later I thought I was going to court to make a plea that day and he called me in and said that he was trying to get Mr. "Capelli" [the prosecutor] to break it down to second degree, and of course it was then that I told him a few of the things that had happened in the grand jury; and I had it written down, and he looked at it and handed it back to me. So whatever it was, he couldn't have felt that it was very important. To me, it was. When he called me back in the day, I thought I was goin in to make a plea, I still didn't know whether I wanted to plead guilty to second degree. I still didn't feel that it was right; I didn't feel I was guilty of that. But by then I was so discouraged with being in that Eastport jail that I was almost tempted, just to get out of there. I mean it's really that bad.

Yeah.

So, when he brought me in, he said that he still had not been able to get Capelli down, and so I asked him, "Well, what are you trying to tell me? In other words, if he will go down to second degree, do you want me to plead guilty to second degree?" And he still didn't say. He said, "Well, I don't know yet."

He hadn't said anything about time yet?

No, and he told me then, "If it goes to trial, the best you can hope for is a second-degree conviction"; so this didn't sound very good.

Which is twenty years to life?

Right. So first or second—what's the difference really? So I went back, and by this time I was working on getting transferred out of Eastport. It just ruined me, really. My nerves were uptight. So I finally got to "Centerville," and then eventually I got called in, and he told me that I was going into court that day to make a plea. I still wasn't sure what was gonna happen. I still didn't want to plead guilty to anything but manslaughter. But if it looked like there was no other choice . . . I don't know, right now I can't say, when I got in front of that judge, whether I would have pleaded to second degree or not. I really doubt it. I was prepared to go all the way to the trial because I just felt there were times in the grand jury when I felt I could have said something, you know, that what they were presenting as evidence I could of shown em something to make it not look quite as bad as it was. Or to make it not look as bad as it looked from the state's point of view. I had been goin over and over things in my mind, and I honestly felt that I could convince enough people on the jury that I was not guilty of first or second degree. But I knew I'd be taking a hell of a chance. But I guess we take a chance every time we get up in the morning whether we're gonna make it to bed that night. So then when I did go to court, I went in Franklin's office, and he said, "I am assuming that you are willing to plead guilty to manslaughter"; and it took me a couple of minutes to realize that he had actually said that. I couldn't believe it.

What couldn't you believe?

That he had got it down to manslaughter. I was expecting that he was gonna fight just to get it down to second degree. And so I told him that I would. I can't deny the fact that I did kill the man; it's a matter of why or how, you know. And there wasn't any point in saying, No, I won't plead guilty on manslaughter, because you gotta get . . . you gotta take something. So, then —oh, yeah, that day he couldn't get me up into the court; so I had to go back, and of course here I was in Centerville and more or less relaxed again. And I had to spend another night in Eastport jail, which happened to be the night they had the sit-in down there. I got involved in that too. Well, not really, but I mean I was there; of course, I didn't sleep all night.

Did Franklin say anything about time?

No.

He didn't say anything?

Well, no, I'll take that back. He didn't say what the prosecutor was gonna recommend. All he did is told me that the maximum was fifteen, and that more than likely the prosecutor would recommend as a maximum the full fifteen. But he didn't say anything about what he might recommend as a minimum. But of course I was still figuring that even fifteen is better than life. From cases that I had heard of or from what people have said, I figured with no previous record that I stood a halfway chance of maybe getting something like seven to fifteen. Oh, when that judge said eleven to fifteen, that was rough.

But Franklin hadn't led you to believe——?

No, he didn't say anything at all. I had sent him a statement from Centerville, right after I made the plea. Actually it was just my . . . what I wanted to say to the judge, but I wanted him to read it first. I was hoping that before I went up there in front of the judge, he would call me in his office and say, "Well, now, this is OK," or somethin like that.

Yeah.

Well, I got called upstairs and, zap, right in front of the judge, [Franklin] kind of leaned over and he said, "Do you want me to read this, or what?" I mean, I didn't really have much of a chance to . . . I didn't even know what he really felt about it. I said, "Well, if it's gonna help me"; and he said, "Well, it might not help you, but it won't hurt you any." So I said, "Well, then go ahead." So he gave it to the judge to read. I don't know. Of course right then it was too late to think about doin it any different way. Like I say I'm unfamiliar with court procedures, but to me, by the judge just reading it to himself, it was like it never became a part of the record or the hearing or anything. Really now, it's just completely lost as far as later parole boards and sentence review, because it's just a piece of paper the judge read and handed back to the lawyer. And then of course when the judge asked me if I had anything that I wanted to say, I said "Well, nothing really except what was on that statement that I made." Mr. Capelli said that by reducing the charge to manslaughter, I had already been given every consideration that I should get, and that he recommends maximum sentence of fifteen years. And Mr. Franklin then said that he realizes that the maximum penalty has to be imposed here because of the crime itself; but he wanted the judge to consider because of my previous record, which I had none, that I be given a lower minimum so that I'd have a chance. Something to work for. So when he got through and the judge asked me if I had anything to say, and I told him, Nothing, he just sat up and read off the sentence like he knew what he was gonna give me before we ever got in that courtroom. And what my lawyer said and what I said didn't mean anything. Just what that prosecutor said.

Why do you think the prosecutor agreed to drop the charge from first degree to manslaughter?

Do you really want to know?

Yeah.

I think to save the state the cost of a trial.

Let me ask you a few questions about Franklin, your lawyer. Did he seem like he knew what he was doing?

Yeah, he seemed to show the experience and the knowledge of it. And I don't really think it's his fault that he can't spend as much time. He's really bogged down. But I also feel that if he believed in—or maybe if he had time to go into it more, he would have felt a little more interested. I don't; I don't think that he really showed the interest that a normal hired attorney would show. Now, of course, I thought this a long time, when I thought he wasn't really showing much of interest or doing much of anything. But he must of showed, he must have done something to get it down to manslaughter. He couldn't have been just sitting around idle; so I can't say that he didn't show some interest.

Thinking back over your dealings with him, do you generally feel that he tried to tell you what to do or took instructions from you?

No, he more or less left it up to me. He made suggestions, but he didn't say, Well this is the way we're gonna do it, and you just be quiet and I'll do all the talking. In fact, when the judge asked me if I had anything to say, he turned to me and asked me if I wanted to say anything else.

Do you think he did a good job for you?

I'd have to say yes.

Do you think he was on your side?

Probably as much as—I don't know; I think he was on the side of the law, which he has to be, naturally. And if he didn't believe in me 100 percent, I don't think he would go against the law to protect me. In other words, I feel he's very capable. If he felt that I were completely innocent, I think he'd probably really fight.

You think he would?

I think so. But—I don't know. To me it sounds like it's kind of a funny situation. I don't understand it a whole lot. But he's on the state payroll, and I don't see how he can go against the state, really. But, of course, it's just like I say: this is part of their job.

If you got in trouble again, would you like to be represented by him?

I don't think that will ever come about, but if something ever did happen, I think if I had the money I'd hire my own lawyer.

Suppose you had some money and you had hired a lawyer—do you think you could have come out of this any better?

Probably not. It could have just cost me money for nothin. All right, let me put it this way: Yes, if I had the money, I think I probably could have got a lighter sentence.

How would that have happened?

Well, I don't know, but I've seen people come in here on manslaughter charges, with previous records both for manslaughter and violence, and come in with sentences like three to ten. And they paid eight . . . between eight and ten thousand dollars for their lawyer. Now there's got to be something there, and this is the same court, and the same judge.

Let me ask you a few questions about the prosecutor: How do you think he saw his job? Do you think he was primarily interested in giving you a fair shake? In punishing you? Getting rid of the case?

His job, I feel, was to get a conviction, and he was gonna get it; and if it meant only a manslaughter conviction, he was gonna get it.

He just wanted a conviction?

Well, now here, again, I never talked to him personally, and I
don't really know that much about him; but I think [what mat-
tered to him was] that I made a statement to the fact that I
had said that I believed I did it. To him—I guess to any prosecutor—this is enough to figure, We've got to convict him of something. In other words, there was no other suspect, you know; it
wasn't a matter of, well, If he didn't, who did? So I think he did
his job to the best of his ability.

Do you think he was fair to you?

I'd have to say yes. I mean if anybody was, say, one way—leaning
to one side or the other—it would have to be the judge himself.
The prosecutor recommended the maximum. This is his job. My
lawyer recommended a low minimum. This was his job. Now
it was up to the judge to decide what he was gonna do.

*What about the judge who sentenced you? Did he seem con-
cerned about your welfare? Hostile? Matter of fact?*

No, I think he was concerned in satisfying the prosecutor. That's
my personal opinion on it.

Well, how do you think he saw his job?

I think he saw his job as a formality. He was there because this is
the way the courts are set up.

The prosecutor really runs the show?

That's the way I look at it; that's the way I see it.

*Why do you think it happens like that? I mean the judge is
presumably independent of the prosecutor; can do whatever the
hell he wants; doesn't depend on the prosecutor for his job.*

No, that's true. Why I don't know. But here again I suppose
that—I mean I pleaded guilty. I don't know what type of reaction he would have had if it had gone to trial or anything.

Do you think the judge was fair?

Well, not in the sense that he didn't seem to take into consideration anything, but just . . . well, now see, here again, it's hard
to say if he was fair. What is fair? I mean is the judge supposed

to consider the person, his previous record, the chances of it ever happening again?

Why shouldn't he?

Or why shouldn't he? Right. That's the way I feel. But to me, now, my presentence investigation—none of it was read in the court; I don't even know what was recommended, but it doesn't seem like very much could have been taken into consideration from that. Cause I know as a fact that the woman that made this investigation . . . she went to visit my mother and stepfather, and they had the impression that she was more or less impressed with my service record and things like that. But the judge's sentence didn't seem to have considered this at all.

Let me ask you a couple of questions about your sentence: Was the sentence you received about what you had expected?

No, it was higher than what I expected, the minimum was higher. I expected about seven to fifteen; I was hoping for maybe a five to fifteen, but I expected about seven.

And this expectation came from talking to other people in jail?

Yeah, that and mostly from past history, cases where other charges, similar—in similar circumstances and so forth.

Do you think it was a fair sentence?

Well, it was within the law.

Suppose you were a judge and a guy came before you who was you, had all your characteristics—what would you have given him?

I would have given probably the maximum, but the fact that it was the first time, and I think I would have tried a little harder to understand the circumstances that led up to the incident, and in doing so make a minimum low enough so that the man had time to get his mind clear and go out and prove himself. I feel once a person is back out in society, if he is going to lead the same type of life he did before and go back into the same things, he's going to wind up right back here. I mean as far as I'm concerned, if the guy gets out and doesn't know enough to stay out, bring him back in and lock him up and throw the key away. But I feel a man should have at least one chance.

So, what would have been a good one—three years, five years?

Oh, five, probably.

Several significant themes appear in this description. First, notice the stress upon the conditions in the jail in which this defendant was held for two and a half months awaiting disposition of his case. The conditions were rotten, not only by his account but also by the admission of correctional officers in charge of the jail. This is not peculiar to Connecticut, but is typical of many states: those being held in "pretrial detention"—those who are presumed innocent of any crime because they have not yet been tried or convicted—are often subjected to living conditions far worse than those endured by persons convicted and sentenced to prison. Not only are the living conditions sometimes abominable, but time hangs heavy on the defendant's hands: this man waited two and a half months; some others waited twice as long. These two facts—the living conditions and the delays that filing of motions or demanding a trial can produce—place strong pressures on the defendant to get it over with, to cop out and "escape" to prison. As this man says: "I didn't feel I was guilty of [second-degree murder]. But I—by then I was so discouraged with being in that Eastport jail that I was almost tempted, just to get out of there. I mean it's really that bad." So, the typical defendant confronts a wait under conditions that are to be avoided. If he wishes to attempt to fight his case (or delay it in hopes of a better deal)—filing pretrial motions, demanding a trial—the wait can go on and on. When we discuss plea-bargaining later, this pressure to "just get out of there" should be recalled.

Relatedly, notice his comments about his attorney. This defendant—like the majority of those interviewed—was represented by a public defender. Public defenders are employed by the state to provide representation for indigent defendants. In Connecticut, and in many other jurisdictions, they are greatly overburdened, handling a volume of cases far beyond their capacity to give any one sufficient personal attention. This defendant got more than his share, for he was charged with a capital offense; most defendants reported spending a total of about five to ten minutes with "their" public defender. But even in the case discussed above, the public defender did not visit the jail. Rather, he typically sees the defendant in the bullpen (lock-up) of the courthouse, in the corridor, in the courtroom. The conversations are brief; they center not around the circumstances and motives of the crime, potential legal defenses, the defendant's needs and desires, but around the "deal"—what can be obtained in return for a guilty plea. The deal and the bargaining that surround it are the centerpieces of lawyer-client relations.

This relationship leads most defendants, including the man quoted above, to wonder whether "their" attorney is on their side. He doesn't spend much time with them; he doesn't seem concerned with them as persons; rather, he is concerned with the disposition. Most conclude that he is not on their side. Contributing to this view is an institutional factor: the public defender is *paid* by the state. To most defendants—even more than to the man quoted above—money is terribly important, and whoever pays the piper calls the tune. If the public defender is paid by the state and the prosecutor is paid by the state, why should they fight, how *can* they fight? As this man noted in discussing his public defender: "He's on the state payroll, and I don't see how he can go against the state, really." This is a common view, and one to which we shall return. Thus, in dealing with *his* attorney, the typical defendant wonders whether the lawyer actually represents him, represents the state, or is a broker or middleman.

What of the prosecutor? His job is getting convictions. He runs the show; the judge generally follows his recommendations. He is seen not as a particularly malevolent figure, nor as a particularly sympathetic figure, but as a man doing his job.

What of the judge? To a large extent he is viewed as an irrelevant man. His is among the easiest of jobs, for he sits there and does what the prosecutor tells him to do. His is the job to which others aspire, for it is prestigious, yet not very taxing. He is not the independent arbiter, sitting magisterially in his robes and mediating between two sides, but a kind of figurehead, a kind of rubber stamp.

What of the sentence? It is prescribed, in broad terms, by the statute books, and within these limits is determined by luck, by bargaining, by what the "going rate" is for a given crime; not by what the offender himself needs, for he is an object or a file, but by what will turn the case over, what will enable the system to go about its business.

What of the law itself? The man quoted above—and almost all with whom I spoke—believe that the laws they violated were good laws, that the acts they performed are deserving of punishment. Their experience with the criminal justice system does not teach them that they ought not kill or rob or break and enter, for they already believe these things. If the man quoted above is released and doesn't kill again, it will not be because he learned this from his experience in court and prison. If the man who breaks and enters gets out and does it again, it will not be because he failed to learn that he *ought* not steal. In this sense the system does not teach defendants lessons about what is moral and immoral conduct.

What of the criminal justice system? The defendant quoted above learned several things: he learned that what begins as one charge often changes to another. He learned, as well, that such changes (and the sentence he receives) do not seem to be the product of a careful consideration of him as an individual—of his motives, characteristics, needs. Rather, they are the products of the needs of the system. Why did they drop first-degree murder to manslaughter? "I think to save the state the cost of a trial." We will see as we examine the experiences of others that the system as it operates in practice is seen by most defendants as an extension of their life on the street. Outcomes do not seem to be determined by principles or careful consideration of persons, but by hustling, conning, manipulating, bargaining, luck, fortitude, waiting them out, and the like. This exploitation of resources is very much like the life on the street that most defendants know intimately.

How well you do in this world depends upon what you've got and how well you use it. The criminal justice system, like the streets, is a game of resource exploitation. The defendant typically has little in the way of resources and doesn't win. He can, though, with luck and skill, lose less than he might. In this way, I want to argue, the system has no real moral component in the eyes of the defendant. It is an extension of life on the street, and the other participants—the police, the defense attorney, the prosecutor, the judge—are themselves playing a game that is perceived as existing on the same moral level as that of the defendant. If the policeman's job is to catch criminals and the prosecutor's job is to convict them, this is about the same as saying that the defendant's job is to break and enter. All are, in the defendant's eyes, about equally immoral.

These, then, are some of the themes I want to develop here. The defendant quoted above—though he had no previous experience—learned these lessons well. Whether these are the lessons that we want to teach defendants is the question that this book seeks to raise.

---

1. Edmund Cahn, *The Predicament of Democratic Man* (New York: Dell Publishing Co., Inc., 1962), p. 30.

2

Arrest and the Police

A defendant's experience with the legal system begins with his contact with police officers, most often at the time of his arrest. Books, movies, and television portray arrest as a dramatic experience, often involving violence or at least the threat of it. Reality, as usual, is somewhat more prosaic. To the defendant, arrest is, obviously, an anxiety-laden experience. If it takes place during or immediately after the commission of a crime, it may even be violent. But more frequently it takes place sometime after the commission of the crime and is a routine, often reasonably amicable affair. Although the arrest itself often comes as a "surprise" to the defendant, it is an event that is not unexpected and is, to some extent, simply an integral element of the life he leads.

This chapter describes the process of arrest and police interrogation as seen by the defendant. To provide a context for the defendants' view of arrest, we also explore in some detail their view of the police. No simple notion or image of the police can encompass the complexity of the way in which these men see police officers. For most of the defendants, the police are not paragons of virtue, but neither are they "pigs" bent upon tormenting and harassing innocent citizens. Rather, the police are viewed as performing a variety of contradictory roles. The policeman is most often described as simply "doing his job," which is to catch criminals. He is a worker, for whom the production ethic dominates: the better he does his job, the more he will be rewarded. At the same time, he is seen as rather inefficient, and most "small-time" criminals, although they will be caught in the long run, can get away with a lot before the day of reckoning.

Because police often are overworked and sometimes lazy, they engage in shortcuts—they cheat, lie, cajole, pressure, and con. Most are viewed as generally honest men, but the production ethic forces them to violate rules in order to do their job. Occasionally one runs into policemen who are especially zealous, out of personal conviction or desire for rapid promotion, and these men will stop at nothing to do their job. These few, along with others overly impressed with the authority that the uniform, badge, club, and gun provide, are not "good" cops and are the subject of fear and contempt.

Police are also seen as adversaries in a game of cops and criminals, and to commit a crime and get away with it provides many defendants with a sense of satisfaction, for they are outwitting or putting something over on an opponent. Finally, the police are seen as performing a valued task: providing order and protecting life and property. This function is viewed as essential to maintaining a decent society and is highly prized by defendants. In part this is because the defendants see themselves as Hobbesian men, existing in a war of all against all and longing for a Leviathan to establish order and tranquility. In part it is because the defendants feel that when they get something (money, a car, clothes, furniture), they don't want someone else coming along and taking it from them—although they themselves do the same thing to others. And, finally, it is because many defendants see themselves and others as subject to passions and needs that must be controlled if anarchy is to be avoided. Many seem to want someone to provide the brakes upon their behavior that they themselves do not possess. The police *could* do this, and to some extent the men interviewed seem to long for it.

This is a complex mélange of images of and feelings about the police. We will try to sort out some of them in this chapter, for they are an important aspect of the relation between the criminal and the legal system.

ARREST AND THE POLICE

The defendants typically encountered one of three arrest situations: arrest on a warrant, arrest on suspicion of criminal activity, or arrest in the act of committing a crime. The first is often routine and involves little excitement, although it may involve surprise. In the second and third, violence is potentially present and sometimes occurs.

Let us begin with a few typical descriptions of the three arrest situations:

ARREST WITH A WARRANT

Well, I was arrested on the seventeenth [of July]. I was in my bedroom reading the paper. There was a knock on the door and I asked who was it. I didn't directly, distinctly hear a voice, but I felt it was muffled, you know, like they didn't really want to say it was the police.

Yeah.

Anyway, I opened the door; they presented their badge and say, I'm narcotics such and such; "we have a warrant for your arrest." So then they come right on in, went in the bedroom, told me to get my shirt on. So, they didn't search the house or anything. They patted me down, and then they—

Did they find anything when they patted you down?

No.

No?

They never found nothin, never found no narcotics on me at all. So then they put the handcuffs on me and took me down.

Did they ask you any questions?

No questions at all; no, they didn't.

You got to the station house. Did they ask you any questions there?

No. I was asked no questions. I didn't see the bench warrant until I got to superior court.

How soon did you go to court? You were at the station, and they locked you up?

Well, see, this is what they do in Eastport. In Eastport you get arrested, and you go to the superior court; you go to the clerk, you don't go to court; you don't appear in front of a judge. You go to the clerk; he read off the warrant and the charges against you, and tells you that your bond has already been set at ten thousand dollars: can you post bond? If you cannot post bond, they set a date when you're supposed to appear in court.

Now this is just after you—the same day you were arrested?

Right; this was all. It was on a Wednesday or Thursday.

Now did the cops tell you your rights—like you didn't have to talk?

No, they didn't; they didn't say nothin.

Did they tell you you could have an attorney?

They didn't say anything.

Did you think of calling up a lawyer?

On my first arrest I didn't call no lawyer; I called—the first thing I called my parents.

Yeah?

All right, they do allow me to make a phone call. All right, I call my parents, and they did the rest from there.

So you went down to the court. He read it off.

Right.

And how soon did you make bond?

About nine days later.

So you're in jail nine days; you make bond, and you get out.

I get out, and then August twelfth they drop another warrant on me. Now this time I just had dropped my girlfriend off at work. I'm drivin down the street; they pull me over and say, "We got a warrant for your arrest"; so I said, "Bullshit, they ain't got no warrant for my arrest; I just got out of jail last month."

Yeah?

So they took me out of the car, put me in the police car, in the detective's car. They searched my car; they search me; they didn't find nothin. Now they didn't show me no warrant, nothin. So I figured it's just a bunch of harassment; so I didn't go for it. I said, "Naw, I know you all bullshitting." I said when they looked in the car, "You're not gonna find nothin"; so then they said, "Well, where you want us to take your car?" I said, "Well, I'm goin over to my mother's house. You can park it there." So they took the car there and took me downtown, and right today I still haven't seen the warrant.

The defendant eventually pled guilty to possession and sale of heroin and received a two-to-five-year prison sentence.

* * *

Well, they come up to the place where I lived and served me a warrant; said I was under arrest for I guess it was breaking and entering, that charge. They took me to the police station.

Did they ask you any questions?

No, they had it pretty well down pat that I did it. They wait till I got to the station first.

This was for B and E?

Yeah.

So they just said, You're under arrest, took you to the station, didn't ask you anything?

Yeah, well, I knew they were after me anyways.

So what happened when you got to the station?

Well, they locked me in a room; they didn't ask me too many questions. The people I was with—they already put statements in on me, and they had picked some of them up. So they had most of their charges.

Did the police tell you that the guys had implicated you, or did you know it already?

Well, I knew one of them did. With what they told me they already knew, and the way they told it to me, they had everything down pat anyway; so someone must have told them.

Did they inform you of your rights?

Well, I already knew them anyways, but they informed me.

Then they asked you about a B and E?

No, well, they asked me about a bunch of things that happened in town. I didn't say nothing at first, but after they came around with this and that and they knew exactly what had happened during this one, and knew exactly what happened in this one, I decided, well, a waste of time to try to plead not guilty to everything.

Now they told you that you had a right to an attorney at this point?

Right.

Did you think about asking for one?

No.

Why not?

Like I say, this isn't the first time I've been in trouble. I mean, because I figured I knew some of the cops there anyways; they usually give it to me straight.

How did they act toward you—I mean were the cops friendly, hostile, matter of fact?

The ones I knew were friendly, and there was one—the sergeant, I guess he was—wasn't too swift; he thought he knew everything.

Now, you didn't ask for an attorney because you didn't think it would do you any good?

Right.

So you made some statements then?

Yeah.

To how many charges? About?

I don't know. There was a few of them, I guess; yeah, I think three or four.

Three or four. So then what happened?

So they took me to "Northville," and I got there, and the rest of the county started coming with their warrants that they had.

This man was eventually charged with and pled guilty to four counts of breaking and entering, five counts of forgery, four counts of obtaining money under false pretenses, and four counts of conspiracy. He received a series of concurrent sentences amounting to two to six years in prison.

In these two cases, as in most similar cases studied, the defendant found the arrest a rather routine matter. None of the parties involved was particularly hostile. The police were simply doing their jobs, and violence was not threatened. The defendant might have been somewhat surprised (e.g., he was unaware that he had sold to an undercover agent or that someone had signed a statement on him), but arrest was not totally unexpected, and was taken as simply part of the life he led.

In all these cases the police had fairly strong evidence against the defendant and had a warrant calling for the arrest of a named person. The defendants felt that they had little chance to fight the charge—the testimony of an undercover agent or a "statement" signed by an accomplice rendered the rest of the proceeding a *pro forma* affair in which there was no chance of winning, but only the possibility of getting the minimum sentence that luck or bargaining might produce. Of course, potentially, they might fight their cases: they might argue entrapment by the undercover agent or attempt to impeach the witnesses who had signed statements against them. But they did not. The second man—and this is very common—took the statement of a codefendant against him as the end of the case. You have the right not to talk, but if someone has "put in a statement" on you, the case is over. We shall see later that this view is intimately related to defendants' past experience with the legal system and to the fact that the lawyers they later obtain are not viewed as much interested in fighting.

ARREST ON SUSPICION

Another group of defendants were arrested soon after the commission of a crime, typically as a result of information that a crime had been committed and of police efforts to pick up likely suspects. Also included in this class were a number of persons charged with possession of contraband (e.g., drugs, weapons), who had been stopped and searched, usually on the basis of a traffic violation or some furtive or suspicious movement that had led the police to intervene. In these situations—especially when the defendant had committed a crime and the police were looking for suspicious persons —the arrest situation was somewhat more tense and involved the threat or use of violence. For example:

Could you tell me something about your arrest? What were you doing?

On my arrest, which was we were to rob into the "Fratkin Jewelers" in "Greenfield," Connecticut. It involved $300,000 with the diamonds.

You did this?

Yes.

You and some other guys?

Yes. The diamonds, which was $300,000 in all stolen—that's what the papers estimated it at—has never been recovered. The judge that went through this case, because my other two friends went to jury trial, said it was more like a movie script—the way it was planned, the way it was done.

So what happened? How did you get arrested? What were you doing?

The car, a '68 Cadillac, which was supposed to pick us up, somehow got lost, and we had to run down the turnpike, and police saw us running down the turnpike.

This is before they knew about the robbery? They just saw you running?

Well, one of the guys that we thought we knocked out—we didn't want to have intention of no violence in this, but the guy did start to scream; this was outside the house. He went to another neighbor's house and called the police and as we were leavin, the police were comin, and I was running down the turnpike, and the state police car pulled up, jumped out, started firin shots at me and my other companion.

Did they tell you to stop before they started shooting?

No, they just fired five shots. In our case there was weapons in our hands at the time, and since we did break into the house while the people was there, they consider us to be dangerous, which as I come to realize now was a pretty vicious thing to do.

So the cops started shooting at you. Did you stop?

I ran into the marsh. I just laid there for about a half an hour, then I got up. I started to move, and the state police officer came down on me; he had his revolver pointed at me and told me if I moved I'd get my head blown off. So I didn't move, but then one of the police officers was—he says he was strucked, but to my knowledge me or my other companion never hit him. I figure that since we did run into a marsh, and it was a very steep hill goin down to the marsh, I believe he fell and split the top of his head open. And since I was caught first—my other companion wasn't caught—and when I did get into the police station, I was handcuffed in the back. I was thrown up against the wall and had to lean forward on my chin, and they frisked me, and then the detective there kicked my feet out from under me. I fell on the floor almost striking my face, and I was jerked back up. He said, "Why did you hit the cop?" I said, "I didn't hit him," and then again I was slapped in the face, and then he took me in a room and slapped me around, punched me in the head, threw me over the table.

Now let me get this straight. When they arrested you, did they tell you what they arrested you for?

Well, I knew I did it; they felt that. I did do it, but there was still a doubt in their minds because I was asked, and I told them that I was cuttin across the marsh at the time, hitchhikin. I told them I was with another fella and two girl companions and I ended up gettin in a fight with one of the guys. I ended up gettin thrown out of the car.

So you think they sort of halfway believed you?

One of the police officers . . . I was dressed—I had a sharkskin suit on, a cashmere coat, white shirt, tie, and everything. Cause I didn't look like the type that would—you know, the guy they were really lookin for.

So they asked you whether you'd been on this job, and you told them the story?

I told them—I was really saying—I didn't say nothin.

Yeah? They asked you questions when they arrested you or after they got to the station?

This is after we got in the station.

Before that they hadn't asked you any questions?

They didn't ask me nothin, just—

Did they tell you about your rights—like your right not to say anything?

They brought me in a room. First they, after they put me back in—they put me in a cell—they came and got me about ten minutes later, and they brought me in the room and told me my rights, told me I had a lawyer, I could have a lawyer, everything like that. And then they told me to take off all my clothes because they were lookin for the diamonds, and they kept my sharkskin suit and my cashmere coat. There was a little bit of blood on it, and they were gonna use this for evidence. Then they gave me some—I guess some clothes—a pair of pants and a shirt they must of had in the police station. I didn't say nothin; so I was put back in the cell. As far as makin a phone call, I didn't even get—. At the time, it was about eleven o'clock that night when I was in this room, and they took me out, and they put me in the cell, and I was there all the way till the next morning about twelve o'clock. They wouldn't let me—I asked to make a telephone call, but they just told me I was a suspect.

Who did you want to call?

I was gonna call my mother and another—have my mother call one of these guys who were involved in this to come out and get me out on bond, because I was on parole at the time.

At this point you didn't know whether any of the other guys had been caught or not?

No. The police officer, he told me, "We think your friend's been hit," which meant as the bullets were fired, because he thinks that he's been wounded and he better tell us [the police] who he is and let us—he might be out there lying dying in the marsh. And I still wouldn't say nothin.

Did the cops say anything about bond at this point?

Ah, the bond. Since I was a suspect, when they wouldn't let me make the phone call, I knew right then and there that even though they knew—well, they had a pretty good idea that I was a person that was involved in this even though I wasn't caught exactly at the scene of the crime; I was say three thousand yards away; I was dressed; there was—none of the diamonds were on me cause the other guy that was with me, he was the one that had them. No weapons or the mask or the gloves that we wore, the people told em we had, they never found. And so they were kind of wondering maybe. At first, like I said, one of the police officers went for my story. But as soon as they notified the Stratford police and asked for my background and they saw that I'd been arrested two times on other cases for robbery with violence, then, ah, that ended their doubts.

Then you were pretty sure that the victim couldn't identify you.

I knew definitely they could not identify me.

So at this point you figured the only way they could tie you up to it would be if one of the other guys copped out or—

If the other one— well, in this case I ended up being state witness. The reason for this was I did make bond—people did get me out on bond. And the deal was that these guys were supposed to get me a good attorney and that I'd go in the courtroom and I'd take all the weight if there was, you know, they found me guilty.

This was the deal with your—the other guys.

Right.

You agreed to take the weight.

Right.

Why?

Well, if they got me a good attorney, this was—

You thought he could get you off light?

Yeah, I felt I could beat it, I could have beat it if they would of got me a good attorney.

As he indicates, this man felt he had been betrayed by his accomplices and eventually turned state's evidence and testified against them at trial. He received a two-to-five-year sentence in prison.

CAUGHT IN THE ACT

Some defendants are apprehended while committing crimes. In these situations, the danger of violence is greatest.

First question is, Will you tell me something about your arrest? What were you doing and what happened?

Well, I was busted for a burglary, like—

What were you doing when the cops came up?

I was coming out of the house, and they shot me.

You were walking out of the house. Did they say anything?

No, they ain't gonna say, you know; they ain't bother [to] say halt. I mean when they said, Halt! Halt! you know, the bullet came right out of the gun. You know, they said, Halt!—pow!

Where did they hit you?

In the hip.

So what happened then?

Then they brought me to the hospital, took stitches, and gimme some penicillin, you know, for infection, and took some X-rays. Sent me back to the jail.

How long were you in the hospital?

About fifteen, twenty minutes.

What happened to the bullet?

It went right through.

I see. How did they happen to be coming up to the house when you were coming out?

Well, they said, I seen you enter this other house that was around the neighborhood, and they was just combing the area.

So at the station after the hospital, did they ask you any questions?

They asked me, they tried, they asked who was with me—stuff like that, going out by myself. They didn't elaborate on it too much. They really were pretty busy filling out files—when I got shot and stuff like that.

So they charged you with breaking and entering?

No, my original charge was burglary.

Burglary.

And when I went to high court, they broke it down.

So at this point you're in the police station charged with burglary? They got you sorta dead to rights.

Yeah.

What happened then? I mean, they didn't need a statement from you, as to whether you'd done it?

Nah, they had a larceny charge on me too. They said they found a hundred dollars on me. I didn't have no money on me at the time. They threw the larceny charge in there. I didn't have nothing on me; then I guess they just—they dropped all that in low court, larceny and resistance charge.

This young man eventually pled guilty to two counts of breaking and entering and received a sentence of one year in jail.

*   *   *

Several observations about the process of arrest may be made. Most emerge in the defendants' accounts discussed above, which are typical of the variety of accounts obtained.

The police appear generally not to engage in a great deal of overt misconduct; for example, physical brutality or manhandling of defendants. Occasionally such misbehavior was reported by defendants: excessive force in making an arrest, or "sweating" a narcotics addict (refusing to give him medication until he made admissions). For the most part, though, the police appear to have gotten the right man and to have handled his arrest with reasonable efficiency.

Relatedly, the police did not usually engage in a great deal of interrogation of suspects about the crime for which they were initially arrested. Usually there was little need: they had already built a case (upon evidence from informers, undercover agents, witnesses, and others) and had a warrant; they found contraband on the suspect, or they caught him in the act. The interrogation that occurred generally dealt with *other* crimes the defendant might have committed, or with attempts to procure information about crimes committed by others. This is viewed by the defendants (probably justly) as a tacit— and sometimes explicit—form of bargaining: in return for admissions which help the police to "clear" (solve) other cases, the defendant will lose little or nothing (he will receive, probably, concurrent sentences) and may gain something for being cooperative. Providing information about others, however, is viewed with distaste: ratting on one's friends is immoral. A defendant will engage in it only when he himself is in dire straits and must do something to meliorate his position, or, more frequently, when he believes that he has been betrayed and provides information as a form of reprisal. The interrogation with an intent to clear other cases does seem to occur frequently and often meets with success, mainly because the defendant believes that he has little to lose in making admissions about other crimes (not infrequently, even admitting to crimes that he himself did not commit).

The men were, for the most part, in fact guilty of the specific crimes for which they were eventually arrested. Only a few protested their innocence, most in an unconvincing manner. But all (with three exceptions) admitted that they were guilty of the *class of crime* for which they were arrested and eventually convicted. That is, the junkie who claimed that he was the victim of the planting of dope or a set of works (narcotics paraphernalia used for cooking and injecting heroin) was invariably in fact a junkie. Even if he protested that in this instance the police had misbehaved, he was in a general sense guilty of the crime of which he was convicted. Relatedly, many of the men who eventually pled guilty to multiple counts indicated that they were guilty of some of them, though not of others. Again, they were in a general sense guilty, for they had been committing that kind of crime. This kind of "general" or "categorical" guilt is of great importance to the defendants themselves, for in some sense they feel that it is acceptable to convict a man for the "wrong" B and E if he was in fact committing B and E's. As many put it, "It was time for me to do some time."

In the theory and rhetoric surrounding our judicial system, arrest is merely the gateway to the legal system; but in the eyes of the defendants, it is perhaps the most important event in the judicial process. For most of the men, the case was virtually "over" when the arrest occurred. After arresting a man, the state still has, at least in theory, many hurdles to clear before that man is convicted and punished: he is presumed innocent, and the state must prove his guilt beyond a reasonable doubt. Furthermore, a series of procedural constraints guard the defendant's rights (e.g., constraints on coerced confessions, illegally obtained evidence, and hearsay). But for the men discussed here, arrest largely settled the case. Once the cops have you, what is of importance is how well you do on sentencing day. In between are a series of way stations: arraignment, setting of bail, often a long wait in jail, bargaining about a guilty plea, the entering of the plea, the presentence investigation. How the defendant behaves along the way—especially his fortitude in waiting "them" out and his skill in bluffing and bargaining—can affect his sentence. In addition, luck plays a large role in the outcome. But what happens in the interim has little to do with anything other than the *sentence*.

This failure to distinguish between arrest and conviction is not entirely surprising. After all, these men *were* for the most part ultimately convicted. Two-thirds of those interviewed ended up in prison, and there seems to have been substantial evidence against most of them. But, as suggested above, this failure to distinguish flies in the face of the theoretical underpinnings and rhetoric of our legal system. The factors that produce it are intimately related to the operation of the system in practice and to the potential impacts that this operation has upon those who become involved in it.

Examining the stories of the men interviewed, we find that a majority of them had some potential legal defense that might have been raised—although it might well not have succeeded. In many drug cases, involving either stopping of suspects on the street or searches of premises without warrants, there appeared to exist—although most defendants either weren't aware of or didn't mention—the possibility of attacks upon the admission of evidence obtained. In drug-sales cases an issue of entrapment sometimes appeared to exist. Finally, and most commonly, the defendant in the station house who was confronted with a "statement" against him usually took this to be the end of the case, making further resistance or denial of guilt pointless. Most of the "statements" against defendants came from coviolators who themselves might have something to gain from implicating others. Presumably those making statements were impeachable witnesses, having prior records and reputations that would lead one to doubt their general veracity. Again, this is not to say that in all or even many cases such a tactic—refusing to admit anything, going to trial and attempting to impeach the witness against the defendant—would have succeeded. But such a possibility generally never occurred to the defendant. Many defendants, indeed, were not aware of the existence of such avenues of defense. Thus, the procedural safeguards available to defendants were, for the men interviewed in this study, largely irrelevant.

A variety of factors contribute to this view. One, discussed in a later chapter, is simply that the defendants feel that their attorneys are not (or will not be) interested in fighting. Another is the feeling, again probably correct, that fighting a case will result in more harsh punishment than will be meted out if one simply acquiesces. This latter view is related to a premise that if they fight they will lose. They will lose because a police officer will always be believed in a conflict of testimony between defendant and policeman. Relatedly, the police are believed to be quite willing to lie in order to convict the defendant. Furthermore, *any* witness for the state will be believed if pitted against a defendant, regardless of who he is or how unsavory his background is. Finally, many defendants know they *are* guilty as charged and are resigned to their eventual conviction. Thus, the defendants' resignation stems from an unawareness of the theoretical workings of the judicial system, cynicism about the way the system works in practice, and the feeling that they "deserve" to be punished.

The defendants generally feel that, once they are arrested, the "moral burden" has shifted. This notion of the "moral burden" is discussed by Jerome Skolnick in relation to the admissibility in court of evidence illegally obtained:

> . . . if something is found, the moral burden immediately shifts to the suspect. The illegality of a search is likely to be tempered —even in the eyes of the judiciary—by the discovery of incriminating evidence on the suspect. For example, when a suspect turns out actually to possess narcotics, the perception of surrounding facts and circumstances about the reasonableness of the arrest can shift in only one direction—against the defendant and in favor of the propriety of the search—even if the facts might have appeared differently had no incriminating evidence been discovered.[1]

As Skolnick suggests, and the defendants notice, the crucial participants in the administration of criminal justice—the prosecutor and the judge—behave as if the moral burden is on the defendant. He is, in their eyes, presumed guilty once he has been arrested. The members of the court system are concerned with factual rather than legal guilt, not with protecting his procedural rights, but with determining his sentence. The defendant himself feels this moral burden, for he is probably guilty and knows that he has done something that he accepts as wrong. His own notions of "categorical" guilt tell him that he deserves punishment, even in those instances in which he confesses to and is punished for some things he did not do.

The mixture of the two factors discussed above—a rational calculation about the probable inefficacy of exercising legal rights because of the structure of the system and a kind of moral resignation—is complex. The latter, however, is crucial. It will also be dealt with in more detail later, for it indicates something of what a defendant has learned from past experience and takes with him into his encounter with the legal system. The system does not teach him that what he has done is wrong, for he already believes that. It does teach him that there is little point to the legal safeguards and procedural protection that are available to him.

In any event, arrest rather than trial is the crucial step in the process from the defendant's perspective. With this in mind we shall now turn to a more detailed discussion of his perceptions of police officers.

IMAGES OF THE POLICE

Most people in our society have a variety of images of what it is like to be a policeman, what policemen themselves are like, and what functions the police perform.[2] We see them as law-enforcement officials. Their presence acts as a deterrent to crime. When a crime has been committed, they seek out the violator and arrest him. Thus, their job is to prevent law-violating behavior and to apprehend those who do break the law. To some, more basically, they are a kind of army, a line of defense against social anarchy, protectors of persons and things against damage by others. In a more symbolic sense, they are the most visible manifestations of public authority, of the existence of laws and the sanctions that can be imposed upon those who violate them. They also perform important social service functions: helping lost children, aiding victims of accident and crime, settling domestic disputes. Most of us also believe that, in addition to performing these varied and valuable social functions, they sometimes abuse their authority: they can enforce law in a discriminatory fashion; they can harass and be unduly brutal; they can be corrupted and become confederates of criminals rather than upholders of law.

For most of us, however, these images are largely the product of inference, of occasional direct observation, and of the presentation of images by various media. Direct experience with a police officer is a relatively rare occurrence; for most of us, the police are present without being experienced.

Criminals experience the police much more directly. The criminal is, like the rest of us, exposed to the images of the police officer found in schoolbooks, literature, movies, and on television. But much more important is his direct experience. More than most people in the society, the criminal sees the police officer as a human being rather than an abstraction. He is familiar with what it is like to be a police officer, with what the job entails, with the complexity of both the role that the policeman is called upon to fulfill and the organizational and personal pushes and pulls that the typical officer encounters.

The various views of the police officer suggested above are all part of the criminal's view of cops, but are tempered by his experience with them. The most important function that the officer is seen as performing is that of law enforcement: catching criminals. Most people would probably perceive the job similarly, but they would be inclined to see it as simply a valued social function. The criminal considers it not so much a valued social function as a *job*. Because it is a job, it is likened to other occupations in our economic system: there is a production ethic, good work (many arrests) is rewarded, and each man is generally attempting to better himself in his organization. Occasionally you encounter a ratebuster—an overzealous officer who tries too hard—but most police officers are simply workers in an organization. This rather down-to-earth view of the policeman's job is summarized in the following remarks of a young man currently serving an eighteen-month-to-three-year sentence for attempted B and E:

> I see them as people following orders, and that's all, you know, like anybody else. They got a job and they do the job, that's all. They don't think about it one way or the other. The majority of them, I think. Some of them are—some of them are oppressive; some of them are fair. But I don't think cops in general, you know, are oppressive. Depends on what type of work, where you work at, where is he working at. The majority of cops I know, or heard of or something like that, are the ones that works around where there's a lot of dope addicts, stuff like that. That's like where I was at mostly. I think the majority of them—not the majority of them, but like technical squad, detective squad— they were, the special group to examine dope addicts and shit, and dope pushers and whatnot. I think they're too serious about their job. They go to all, all kinds of extremes to catch people on anything. They do anything to catch you. But in fairness, you know, like a regular cop, blue suit, they ride through the neighborhood and just ride through. In a slum he's riding

through there looking for trouble. And if it's in like a section of town where it's all houses, and people living there own their own house, he might ride through to catch somebody doing something in there that don't belong there or just riding through, have somebody want some help, they stop. Just patrol duty; they gave them a beat.

Well, do you think when he rides through the ghetto, he's looking for trouble?

No. I don't think he's looking for trouble. I think he's riding through the ghetto cause like his superior officer told him to take that beat. I think that, really, most cops would rather ride through like section of town where it's all houses and all people work all day, all the people work all day. You know, the men work, the women is home. I think they would rather have a job like that, working a job, whereas dope and shit, cause like it's less work. I think just like anybody else, they don't want to work.

Their job is seen as a rather difficult one: there are many more criminals than policemen; there is danger in police work; and most people don't like cops. In addition, like other workers, most policemen are inclined to do the least possible work and hence to take shortcuts. They are not perceived as especially efficient in doing their jobs. Most crimes can be gotten away with, though in the long run you will be caught—not because of the zealousness of the police but because of bad luck, a buddy who rats you out or some carelessness.

This view of the police officer as a worker is important. It makes much of his behavior understandable to the criminal, and it places boundaries upon what behavior can be expected from the typical officer: he will do his job so long as it doesn't involve overexerting himself, and he won't go out of his way to look for trouble.

The difficult police officers are those who are extremely zealous. In one city in Connecticut, for example, a narcotics detective is almost legendary and generally hated. This has resulted from his apparent zeal in catching junkies and dealers. He is reputed to engage frequently in illegal practices, such as the planting of dope and random searches. He is even reputed to have arrested his mother at one point in his career. The hostile reaction that he engenders from the drug community is the product not so much of his alleged illegal activities as of his zeal. He is, as suggested above, viewed as something like a ratebuster on a production line. He doesn't accept or abide by the informal rules that are supposed to govern relations between cops and criminals. The enmity that his activities engender seems related to the fact that he apparently cares so much, that he doesn't exhibit the typical workmanlike indifference that is the norm, and hence his behavior is to some extent hard to understand and to predict. Many defendants volunteered speculations about his motivation —dealing with his childhood—indicating that they had considered *why* he might be the way he was. Policemen such as this man—ones who are viewed as exceptionally zealous in law enforcement or as abusing their authority to fulfill personal needs for power—are the subject of intense hatred by those interviewed. The average policeman is not hated: he is simply doing his job.

Clearly, to a man who regularly engages in criminal acts, the policeman just "doing his job" is not the same as the garbage collector, the schoolteacher, the factory worker, all of whom are also doing their jobs. For the policeman represents the power and authority to take away the criminal's freedom, to put him through much misery. Thus, the cop-as-worker threatens the criminal-as-worker. This latter phrase is meant seriously. Most of the men I spoke with were not "professional" criminals who depended upon crime for a living, but they did engage in large numbers of criminal acts. Especially if they were junkies, they committed crimes regularly. Even those not on dope led lives that involved numerous law violations: they fought a lot, got drunk, stole cars, occasionally pulled B and E's. Their lives were defined by much law-violating behavior. Thus, they had a special relation to the police.

In part this relation was similar to a kind of amicable competition between two businessmen: they were working on the same territory and competing for the market. The criminal obviously does not want the policeman to control the territory, for he will be put out of business and likely in jail. But he doesn't *hate* his competitor—so long as he competes honestly—rather he sees him as simply an adversary in a system that in many ways resembles a game.

Most of the men I spoke with were regular law violators, and many took pride in the success of their illegal endeavors:

Do you think a guy can just get away with crimes indefinitely?
If he's bright enough?

Yup.

What do you think about that? Is it a good thing or a bad thing?

It's good.

It's good?

I think it's quite an achievement, really.

Few were as explicit as this, but most implied that there was some satisfaction in success at crime, and that satisfaction turns in part on beating a "them" that is embodied by the police. Thus, "being slick" is one of the most potent accolades that a person can gain. A "slick dude" gets away with things; he beats the system. He is the man who never has the dope on him, the man who, though his house is searched six times, can say with pride that they never found a thing even though he was regularly dealing in drugs.

The combination of viewing the policeman as a worker doing his job and the importance attached to the slick dude produces (from a libertarian perspective) somewhat anomalous views about police misconduct, such as planting dope on a junkie or on a dealer who can't be caught legitimately. This type of behavior does not produce unequivocal righteous indignation. Rather, it is generally viewed with a kind of resignation, sometimes a kind of petulance, and sometimes with a touch of pride. Consider a junkie who is selling drugs to support his own habit. The police know that he is doing it, but he is extremely slick. He is careful about his customers and does not become involved with undercover agents. He stashes his stuff in unexpected locations and is never successfully searched by the police. Finally, the police stop him one day and search him, and, as usual, find nothing. The police officer then produces a few bags of dope and says to the suspect: "These are yours." The defendant is arrested and booked for possession and eventually cops out because he feels that the officer will be believed if he testifies that the search was legal and produced the dope.

Many of us would say that this is among the most flagrant abuses of police authority. Others would be less sure since the man was in fact guilty of a heinous crime and belongs in jail, though rules had to be bent, even violated, to put him in jail. The defendants I spoke with would find this situation—and they feel it is not infrequent—somewhat problematic. First, they would acknowledge that in some sense the officer had done something improper, for he shouldn't plant dope on suspects. At the same time, they feel that the officer *has* to do it, or at least that it is easily understandable why he did: his *job* is to catch that defendant, and it must be difficult—if not intolerable—to know he's guilty but not be able to catch him. Likewise, the defendant reasons: I know it's wrong to steal, but I do it when I've got to have something or want something badly. Finally, it is to some extent a badge of accomplishment to be set up in this way. It is an indication that the criminal was too slick to be caught fairly; so he merited some special attention. Clearly, the defendant or another criminal who observed these events does not like what happened and does not like jail. But the confusion they exhibit—the lack of unequivocal indignation that the detached libertarian would be able to muster—is an indication of a particular view of law violation, due process, and the function of the police. It is useful to note that if the person upon whom dope was planted was *not* a junkie or if a man arrested for robbery or assault is viewed as having been the subject of a mistake—and is not himself a robber or assaulter—then the defendants would voice righteous indignation. This situation presents for them clear wrongdoing and injustice; the previous case is more a mixed bag. As suggested above, this ambivalence about police and police misconduct is a product of the recognition of the policeman-as-worker and his production ethic, the gamelike nature of the relationship between policeman and criminal, and the confusion in our society between the concepts of factual and legal guilt.

This view of the policeman as an adversary seems to be more than simply the product of the fact that the men interviewed were, at the time of their latest arrest, engaged in a significant amount of law-violating behavior, which naturally put them at loggerheads with the law-enforcement aims of police officers. A view of the police as adversaries seems to have roots that extend far back into the lives of many of the men interviewed. The questions asked of the men included the following: (1) "Think back to the time you were a kid—

say, six, eight, ten years old—what did you think about police then?" (2) "Can you remember the first time you ever had contact with a policeman? What was it like?"

The responses to the first question were mixed. Many of the men responded in ways that are probably common: they thought policemen were "good" men who stood for authority and justice and also saw them with a tinge of fear, for they represented power. Several of the men volunteered that they, like most kids, had wanted to be police officers when younger. But a large number responded that they had never liked cops, had always feared them, and had seen them as men to be avoided. This may be, in part, simply a kind of retrospective rationalization: their later experience with police officers colored their views and made them cast their recollections in negative terms. Still, more than most people, I think, these men, even as children, saw police officers not as helpers and good guys, but as a kind of "they" who possessed a power over their lives that was resented.

This view is related to their experiences with police officers as children. In the initial discussion in this section of the functions of police officers, we mentioned social service functions: helping lost children, directing traffic, assisting in the resolution of domestic disputes. These appear to be salubrious activities in the abstract, but may be less so if one is himself the subject of such "service." A "lost" child—if he is outside his neighborhood—may to the police officer be initially the subject not of compassionate interest but of suspicion. Directing traffic in the inner city may involve clearing the streets of children using them as playgrounds. Settling a domestic dispute may involve siding with one parent or another in front of a child, or appearing to interfere with family life, or embarrassing a child by having his parents' discontents become the subject of notice by outsiders. Thus, many of the social service functions performed by police officers —well intentioned and necessary though they may be—were subjects for hostility to many of the defendants when they were children.

Even more striking were the reports of first remembered contact with police officers. Again, the problem of retrospective reconstruction must be noted, but the reports were still impressive. About one-third of the respondents answered in ways that might be expected: they remembered the policeman on the beat or directing traffic; or they recalled seeing the officer's uniform and badge and being impressed; or they had a neighbor who was a cop. The rest of the respondents, though, spoke of brushes with the law, often at very early ages (typically six to ten years old). Their first contact occurred when they had stolen a bike or been caught shoplifting. Even more striking was the large amount of random and apparently purposeless lawbreaking that led to the man's first recalled contact with a police officer: breaking windows, setting fires, pulling fire alarms, and the like. Examples of initial experience with police officers include the following:

> When I was about seven or eight, I pulled the fire alarm, and the cops came to my house.
>
> *How did they treat you?*
>
> Treated me all right, you know. They just talked to my mama and father. Hey, I was just a little kid.
>
> *So, as far as you could tell, they were pretty good guys?*
>
> No, I didn't like them, because they came to my house and ratted me out. So I guess that's when I started disliking them.
>
> *When was the next time?*
>
> When I started stealing cars and stuff.
>
> *How old were you then?*
>
> About fourteen.
>
> *And why did you do that?*
>
> I did it cause I caught the talk; it seemed how I always hung around with the bad guys, you know. Never hung around with the squares. I always had to be superhip. I always hung around with the superhip crowd. I learned all my shit from them, you know; so you swung out with the superhip, you had to be superhip. So I guess stealing cars and doing what they did was cool.

*   *   *

> *When's the first time you can remember ever talking to a police-man or having some contact with one?*
>
> When I got in trouble.

How old were you?

About seven.

What was it about?

I don't remember. I know I got in trouble when I was really young, stealin money and stuff.

Did the police treat you okay?

What can they do to a little seven-year-old kid? Can't put him in jail.

* * *

When I was about seven . . . was around the school around nine o'clock, we was havin a rock fight; some people complained, some of their windows was being broken.

The complexity of the experiences and attitudes of defendants-as-kids is summarized in the following exchange:

Why do you think people lose respect for the police? Because they get caught?

Yeah, they figure well—a lot of them look at it with the philosophy, well, this guy that goes out and B and E's a house or steals a car is not directly hurting this person, this policeman; so why does this policeman have to stick his big nose into it and be a hero and catch this kid.

Did you feel that way?

At first, yeah. But now, you know, I'm a little older, not a whole lot older, but I'm seventeen years old. I should be starting to think about things that seemed—some things as they really are.

How do you feel about policemen?

They're doing their job, that's all there is to it.

Do you respect them, do you think?

To a degree, yes. There are some glory seekers, you know, and stuff like that, and big shots who just like to really make things rough.

A couple of years ago you think you had less respect for the police than you do today?

Yeah.

Well, what about when you were a little kid?

It wasn't respect, it wasn't respect when I was a little kid. It was lots of things . . . I think looking at it from almost an infantile point of view. You know, you see their blue uniforms, and you automatically relate it with a jail; so I think it was more or less fear rather than respect, and a lot of times a uniform can mean something when you're small—not respect, but you might like the idea of the uniform. Wow, that really looks cool, and so on. I think I'll be a cop when I grow up so I can wear a blue suit.

Did you think that when you were a kid?

Yeah, when I was about five years old. Just like you have fantasies about being a fireman and stuff like that. But then as you grow older, things—your mind changes. You might still not see it from a realistic point of view, but you'll look at it a little bit more objectively, and from fear it then turns into respect; from respect it takes a vast jump and turns into contempt.

Now what causes that jump do you think? The jump in perspective?

Age, semimaturity, a contempt of all authority—it starts with your parents and goes right on up to the president of the United States. It's just a natural rebellion that starts in the beginning of puberty, I think, and ends maybe about sixteen years of age in normal maturing process. Now I don't feel any contempt for the police, I really don't. They're just doing their job, and that's all there is to it.

No doubt some psychological or sociological explanations for the behavior of the defendant-as-kid and the run-ins with the law which his behavior produced might be offered. Suffice it to say here that the experiences reported by most defendants-as-kids are quite similar to their current lives: their ways of living, their day-to-day behavior, involved them in activities which led to the intervention of police officers. Their current views of the police not as helpers but as adversaries have roots in their experiences since childhood. In their lives, "being a kid" often involved activities—stealing, trespassing, random acts of vandalism or violence—that produced conflicts with police officers.

Thus far we have discussed the variety of images of police officers that seem to characterize the defendants: a view of the policeman-as-worker, whose job it is to enforce the criminal laws; the cop as an adversary in a game of cops and robbers; the policeman as an authority figure, whose job brings him into direct conflict with the day-to-day behavior of the defendant.

In none of these roles does the policeman command the *respect* of the defendants. He has his job to do and is generally tolerated as a human being just like the criminal; he is simply a part of life and to some extent is feared. Because the policeman is simply a worker, because he sometimes violates rules (as any worker will), because he is an adversary, he is viewed by the defendants as operating on essentially the same *moral level* as criminals:

> Well, it's not that I don't like em, you know; because they have a job to do. I don't disrespect the man for being a policeman—no, no, not at all. He got a job just like I had a job. My job was selling heroin and gettin away with it and keepin him away from me so I could sell this heroin and stay high, and that was it. And I respected him for being a policeman, and in the same token I expected him to respect me for being [me].

The police—in the eyes of the defendants—are not much better than they are. The expression "every cop is a criminal" has powerful meaning for the defendants: not in the sense that they believe that police officers are especially dishonest or on the take or that they violate laws, nor in the sense that the defendant's criminal behavior is proper, but simply that, although they have the law on their side, their manner of behavior and law enforcement leaves the defendants little to choose between themselves and the police. The same is held to be true for judges and prosecutors: principles do characterize the criminal code; they do not, in general, characterize its enforcement.

There is a final element in the defendants' views of the police that seems of interest, though it is highly speculative. In the defendants' accounts of their crimes and in their discussion of the nature and function of law, many seemed to view man as the prey of his own emotions, drives, and needs. This notion has both individual and social components. Socially, many of the men seem to see themselves in a state of nature, in a war of all against all in which law is a potential restraining device. For example, all were asked whether the law they violated was a "good" law, whether such behavior ought to be punished. With the exception of some convicted of narcotics violations, all said they believed that the law they violated was a good one—that robbery, or assault, or breaking and entering, or car theft ought to be punished. Moreover, all were asked what they thought would happen if the law against their crime did not exist. Almost all suggested that repeal of the law would result in an epidemic of such behavior—everybody would begin stealing from one another, would engage in assaults upon those they didn't like.

To a large extent, then, they tend to see themselves as members of a society in which man's impulses are to take from others, to settle differences by force, in which the weak—unless protected by some outside authority—will be brutalized by the strong. The law—the social contract—places constraints upon such behavior and sets up mechanisms to protect persons and their property from the rapacity of others. The defendants—including those who regularly engage in theft or robbery—recognize this purpose of the law and endorse it. After all, they say to themselves, when I get rich, I don't want someone coming around and taking my property. I'd like there to be a cop and a law for him to enforce to make sure that I'm not victimized in the same way that I myself victimize others.

They not only see themselves as surrounded by persons aching to victimize them if they were worth victimizing, but also recognize themselves as victimizers. When asked why people violate the law or why they themselves did it, most expressed confusion. For some, the answer was simple: they were drug addicts and had to commit crimes to support their habit. But it was apparent that when considering others who were not junkies, they were at a loss to come up with explanations. Moreover, it seemed that they viewed themselves as likely to engage in crime, whether or not they were addicts. In a later chapter, we will discuss their views on the causes of crime. Here, we may note that they fixed on such things as drug addiction, economic conditions, bad childhood or upbringing, an inability to control one's temper, or simply bad luck or fate. Many felt that these were inadequate explanations that didn't get very far in understanding human behavior. They longed for explanations for their own behavior and melioration of their condition; for although a life of crime can have its gamelike qualities, and although for some there is satisfaction in getting away with it, few really *want* to live this way.

Regardless of the possible solutions to their problems, it is important to note that their views of the police—and other law-enforcement workers—are in a sense colored by their own desires to have some external controls placed over their behavior. They see themselves and others like them as basically motivated by self-interest and greed; they would embrace effective mechanisms to control their and others' behavior. In a sense, I think they view the police as having failed them, as being in fact all too human and fallible. They wish that the police were better than they, for the police and the law they enforce seem to have the potential for solving the defendants' personal difficulties in controlling themselves. The failure of the police to do so—the ease with which they can "get away" with something—is itself troubling. On the one hand, it is desirable, for it is a way in which they can "achieve" in a society which provides them with few other avenues for success, and it is a source for relatively easy and quick acquisition of money to fulfill their wants. On the other hand, one can detect a kind of regret in their feelings about the police, for they see themselves as at the mercy of their own demands and would like someone to provide the controls that they find themselves incapable of imposing. In many ways, I think that the contempt for police that many defendants feel is in part a product of their feeling that the police fail to do their job well enough.

This, then, is an initial foray into the defendant's view of the legal system. We have discussed the process of arrest and found it to be a relatively routine matter: the crucial access point to the assembly line of justice, but a matter with which they are quite familiar and which they have come to expect. We have examined the defendants' views of the police and found in them a mélange of often apparently conflicting images and attitudes. The crucial aspect of this discussion —and a recurring theme of this work—is the notion that the policeman (like his counterparts in the later stages of the process from arrest to sentencing) is himself simply doing a job and is the subject of motives and desires that are not markedly different from those of the defendant. The policeman is basically a worker, not an impartial arbiter or enforcer. The process of arrest and the activities of police in general are not so much different from street life itself. You get by; you do what you have to to survive; you take shortcuts; you play games with each other. Nobody is neutral or detached or impartial; everyone has his job and he does it. Dealing with people as individuals rather than as objects or adversaries is not a part of the system, for the production ethic and the organizational structure militate against it.

---

1. Jerome Skolnick, *Justice Without Trial* (New York: John Wiley & Sons, Inc., 1966), p. 221.

2. See Herbert Jacob, "Black and White Perceptions of Justice," *Law and Society Review*, VI (1971), 69–89, for a discussion of racial differences in views of the police and courts.

3

From Arrest to Disposition

Arrest and the placing of charges against a defendant are but the first episodes in his journey through the legal system. Later events determine whether he emerges a convicted criminal or a free man. A brief description of the formal structure of the proceedings in Connecticut from the time of arrest will serve as a preface to a discussion of the defendants' views of what happens to them.*

Immediately after the filing of charges, bond is set for defendants not charged with capital crimes. If court is in session, the defendant is taken there immediately for the formal arraignment. If court is not in session, bail is set by the police or by a bail commissioner. If the defendant can make his bond, or is deemed eligible for release upon his own recognizance, he is released pending the disposition of his case. If he cannot make his bond, he remains in custody, held in one of several jails serving various parts of the state. The conditions in many of the jails (which are used for pretrial detention and for convicted prisoners sentenced to less than a year) are admitted by all—including correction administrators and public officials—to be

* The Connecticut court system has subsequently undergone some reorganization, with an expansion of the jurisdiction of circuit court, though the basic structure described here remains.

odious, much worse than those in the prisons. Thus, the pretrial detainee—who is presumed innocent because he has not yet been convicted of anything—is forced to wait out the disposition of his case in conditions substantially more unpleasant and demeaning than those afforded to convicted criminals.

Connecticut has a two-tiered trial court system. The lower courts are called circuit courts and the higher courts superior courts. Circuit court has jurisdiction over misdemeanors (in general, crimes having a maximum penalty of one year or less) and concurrent jurisdiction over some less-serious felonies, should the prosecutor and the judge choose to exercise such jurisdiction. Most felonies are under the jurisdiction of superior court. Shortly after his arrest, a person charged with a felony is presented in circuit court for arraignment—the formal lodging of charges. In addition, the defendant is entitled to ask in circuit court for a "probable-cause" hearing and to file motions asking for the dismissal of his charges and the suppression of evidence that is alleged to have been obtained illegally. Thus, circuit court serves for felonies as a kind of clearinghouse, putatively making sure that those who are sent on to superior court for disposition—the legal phrase is "bound over" to superior court—have not been arrested and charged frivolously or illegally.

The filing of motions in circuit court and the exercise of the right to a probable-cause hearing are fairly rare occurrences. Usually the appearance in circuit court is a brief one in which the defendant is arraigned and waives his right to a probable-cause hearing. In waiving such a hearing, the defendant is, potentially at least, giving up something important. The probable-cause hearing—in which the state must present sufficient evidence against the defendant to justify his being bound over to superior court for disposition—can be a useful "discovery" device. That is, even if the state has a substantial case against a defendant and "probable cause" is likely to be found, the defense, by forcing the state to present part of its case, can learn the nature of the evidence against the defendant—where the state's case may be weak, what types of defense tactics may be effective in superior court. As noted, this discovery tool is frequently waived by defendants and their lawyers. Most defendants are represented in circuit court by public defenders—lawyers employed by the state to represent persons who cannot afford their own attorneys. Public defenders in circuit court are burdened with heavy caseloads, have little time to spend with each client, and have access to police arrest reports and know the strength of the prosecution's case. Hence, they are typically aware that a probable-cause hearing will not result in dismissal of the case, and they cannot afford to spend much time on such activity.[1] Finally, and perhaps most importantly, the circuit court public defender realizes that the vast majority of his clients charged with felonies whose cases are eventually disposed of in superior court will end up pleading guilty. Thus, discovery of the evidence against him is often viewed as relatively unimportant.* The typical defendant is advised to waive his right to a probable-cause hearing. In return for giving up this right, he is usually offered a reduction in his bail. Hence, a bargain is reached: in return for waiving the probable-cause hearing, the defendant is given a better chance to get out of jail on bond.

Once he is bound over to superior court, the defendant must enter a plea to the charge. Typically, he goes to superior court several times before a plea is actually entered. If he is indigent, his initial appearance results in the appointment of the public defender serving superior court as his counsel. He then shuttles back and forth from jail (or comes in from the streets if he has made bail) until finally he is asked to plead. During this period he has some contact with his attorney. If he is being represented by a public defender, this contact usually comes in the hallways or lock-ups of the courthouse on the days he is called to court. During this period, bargaining about a guilty plea occurs. The defendant's attorney transmits offers from the prosecutor concerning the sentence he will receive in return for a plea of guilty.

He eventually appears before the judge to enter his plea. If he pleads not guilty, a date is set for trial, and he is returned to jail or goes back on the streets. If he enters a plea of guilty, the judge asks him a series of questions concerning his plea. Although they may vary a bit from case to case, the questions generally include the following: Are you pleading guilty because you are guilty? Are you aware of the maximum sentence for the crime to which you are entering a guilty

---

* This may in some respects be a self-fulfilling prophecy: the lack of discovery makes it more likely that the defendant will in fact cop out, for weaknesses in the state's case will not emerge at a pretrial stage.

plea? Were you coerced into pleading guilty or offered anything in return for it? Are you satisfied with the representation afforded you by your attorney? The appropriate responses must be given: Yes. Yes. No. Yes. In many cases the defendant's answer to the question about coercion or deals is a lie: the defendant has been told that the prosecutor will recommend (and that the judge is nearly certain to impose) a particular sentence in return for the plea. But the litany must be gone through, and the plea is then accepted.

The defendant is then typically remanded to custody or bail for two weeks pending a presentence investigation conducted by the probation department. He then appears before the judge and sentence is imposed.

The bargaining that occurs—and it occurs frequently—can center around either charge or sentence. A defendant charged with robbery with violence may eventually plead guilty to simple robbery; a charge of assault with intent to kill may be reduced to aggravated assault; burglary may be broken down to breaking and entering. The charge is of importance, for it determines, to some extent, the maximum sentence that a defendant can receive. If he is sent to prison, the minimum term (e.g., on a two-to-five-year sentence, the two-year minimum) determines the date of his eligibility for parole. The maximum is important too, though less so, for it affects his eligibility for discharge from parole after he is released.

Even more frequent is bargaining over the sentence to be imposed. For most crimes the judge has discretion to impose any sentence up to the maximum permitted by statute. Thus, breaking and entering can be penalized by five years in prison or by a lesser sentence (e.g., two to five years). In addition to bargaining over the sentence for a particular offense, many defendants have been charged with several crimes; for example, eight counts of B and E, nine counts of forgery. In theory a plea of guilty to each count could result in a series of terms in prison for each count. In the plea-bargaining process a defendant may be offered an agreement about a series of concurrent sentences: the eight counts of B and E will produce eight concurrent sentences of two to five years in prison.

In this and the next two chapters, we will discuss the process in more detail: the choices that the defendant feels he has available to him, his view of his relationship with his attorney, and the ways in which he interprets the behavior of the prosecutor and the judge. This brief account suggests the structure of the proceeding: the formal appearances in court, and the informal bargaining that underlies and in many ways determines the results that these formal appearances produce.

To begin to flesh out the reality of the process—as seen by the defendant—let us listen at length to two defendants. They represent somewhat different experiences: in one the defendant was relatively passive, and events simply occur; in the other the defendant engaged in an extensive variety of tactics and bargained actively.

The first man was arrested and charged, on complaint of his girlfriend, with assault with intent to rape. He refused to make a statement to the police. In discussing his case, he indicated that he was probably guilty of assault, but not assault with intent to rape. The report of a "double-cross" by the public defender was not typical, but neither was it uncommon.

> I got arraigned before the judge and got ten thousand dollars bail, and then I stayed in jail ever since then.
>
> *Now, did you intend to plead not guilty to this charge?*
>
> Yes, I was gonna plead not guilty.
>
> *So you were arraigned: they gave you a bond you can't make; so you're back in jail.*
>
> Right.
>
> *What happens then?*
>
> I just stayed there and kept going back and forth to court.
>
> *What did you go to court for?*
>
> For the same charge.
>
> *What was happening?*
>
> The lawyer didn't seem to be doing nothin. Every time I'd go there he would—he wouldn't, he wasn't sayin nothin.
>
> *He was a public defender?*
>
> Yes.

Did you appear in circuit court? Did you have the probable-cause hearing?

Naw, he said it's better not to have it.

So you were bound over?

Yes. To high court.

So you had a different public defender in superior court?

Yes, I had a different one there.

Now, when was the first time you met him?

It was about three months.

You were taken over to superior court, and you met the public defender?

Yes. See, I had started off with "Moore"; then they switched me to some other guy. And none was takin interest in—

Did any of them ever come visit you in jail?

Naw.

The only time you saw them was in the bullpen or around court?

Yes.

Did you eventually plead guilty?

Yes, he told me, "With your record and stuff, you'd better plead guilty."

Who told you that?

The lawyer.

And this is one day in court?

Yes. He told me I would probably get a year; that's why I pleaded guilty.

Did he first ask you what you wanted to plead?

Yes. I said, "I want to plead not guilty; I'm not guilty of it." And then—see I'd been in prison before; so he says, "Well, you take this to a jury trial, you might get a lot of time." He had me pretty scared. So he said, "You better—I think I can get you a year." So I said OK, and then I got up there, and I got five years.

You got the feeling he wanted you to plead guilty?

Yes.

And when he said, "I think I can get you a year," did he say he'd talked to the prosecutor about it, or—?

Yes, he said the prosecutor wasn't gonna recommend nothin. In other words, he wasn't gonna recommend I got time or nothin. But when I got up there in court, the prosecutor recommended I go to prison and aw, everything changed, you know.

Do you think the lawyer thought you were innocent or guilty?

I think he thought I was innocent, but he just didn't want to go into too much trouble. He asked me, "You got any money?" I told him no.

The implication was if you had some money, he'd do a better job for you?

Yeah, he says, "Have you got any money you can give me?" I said, "No, I haven't got no money."

Did you go first to plead in the superior court, and then there was a presentence, and then you got sentenced? or did they do it all at once?

No, I went down there about three or four different times. Pled not guilty, and then I went down there once, and nothin happened—didn't even get to see the judge—and then back again.

To plead guilty?

Yeah, they just kept runnin me back and forth, hopin you get sick of waitin there and then plead guilty.

If you had to pick out a sort of crucial factor that changed your mind from the time you were going to plead not guilty to the time you decided to cop out, what was it?

I started thinking—you know, I did have a prison record, and I really didn't want to plead guilty to that attempted rape, because with the statement he had and everything, I should have got off. And it was really mixed up. I didn't try to run. I could have left the house. I waited there; I thought I was just gonna get threw out [by the police officers].

You were charged with attempted rape or assault with intent to rape?

Assault with intent to rape.

Yeah. At one point you thought you could beat that.

Yeah.

But then you changed your mind.

Yeah, well, when I see he didn't try to do nothin—the lawyer he just got up there and say, "Yes sir, yes sir." He didn't even try to argue with the judge. I figured I'd better plead guilty here, or else I'm gonna get a lot of time.

Now, you got two to five?

Two to five.

If the lawyer had come to you and said, "I'll get you two to five," would you have pled guilty?

I don't think I would have, no.

So it was the fact that he said he could get you a year?

He said he could get me a year there.

And you thought that was a pretty good deal?

Yeah, I figured better than going to prison [i.e., a year in jail is better than a longer term in prison].

Now, thinking about this from the time you were arrested till the time you got sentenced, if you had it to do over again, would you do it different?

Yes.

What would you do?

The first thing I'd do is probably get in contact with my family, get my own lawyer. I'd never believe that lawyer again, never. They'd never give me no public defender; I wouldn't take him.

The next young man was charged with two counts of burglary (carrying a potential maximum sentence of twenty years on each count), one count of resisting arrest, and one count of larceny. He was apprehended and shot by police officers in the course of one of the breaks and placed under a bail of ten thousand dollars by police officers. He asserted that he could have made the bond, but a parole violation warrant had been lodged against him, making him ineligible for release.

So you went to court the next day?

Yeah, I went to court, and they presented the charges. Then they continued it.

Did you have a lawyer when you went to court the next day?

No, I had a public defender.

Did you talk to him at all?

Yeah, he ran the facts and all that stuff. You know, how much time they carry and stuff like that.

How did you intend to plead at that point?

He said that if I pleaded guilty, they drop resistance and larceny and bound the two burglaries over to superior court.

He said they would do that?

Yeah.

He said you ought to do that?

Yeah.

So did you do it?

Yeah.

Were you guilty of both of them?

No, just one.

The other one you were innocent of?

Yeah.

Did you tell them that?

No.

How come?

I mean yeah, I told them, yeah.

You told them. What did he say?

He say nothin. He just said, "It's up to you." I guess he thought I was lying.

So why did you plead guilty to the second one that you didn't do?

Cause I knew if I'd a went to high court that they would eventually break it down to a breaking and entering without permission. Cause I was planning on getting my own lawyer, but then I was gonna see what my public defender was gonna do first.

So the deal he offered was, Plead guilty to two burglaries. They'll drop the resisting and the larceny.

Yeah.

And then what happens? Did he say they'd knock it down to B and E in superior court?

No, he just said they bound it over.

So you waived the probable-cause hearing?

Yeah, I waived it.

And you pled guilty to the one you didn't do because you figured they'd drop it eventually anyway?

No, they'd break it down for a misdemeanor, breaking into without permission. If the public defender wasn't going to do it—if he didn't want to hear it, I figured eventually he'd make a deal because, you see, I waited four months to go to court. I was in the state jail, and from state jail I went to "Northport"—the hospital.

Drugs?

No, suicidal. And I laid up there for a while, and then I came back and went back. I was doing this just to———

You were purposely delaying the superior court case?

Yeah.

Figuring that they'd break it down?

No, well, see at that time the superior court in Eastport was real crowded. You come in there with a case, and they wanted to dispose of it as quick as possible, see. So I figured if I kept on delaying and delaying and delaying, they'd eventually break it down, you know what I mean. He'd come up with some kind of a deal. I sorta like pressed him to come up with a deal, and he came up with a deal.

Who's he?

"Franklin."

The public defender?

Yeah.

This is the public defender in superior court?

Superior court, yeah.

Well, when did you first run into him?

The day I went to superior court.

And this was shortly after you were bound over? How long between the time you were bound over and you first went to superior court?

Well, I was bound over at superior court. I didn't know I—I didn't know when I was going to superior court; so what I did —you know, I cut up [attempted suicide].

Yeah.

And they sent me to [the hospital], see. So then from [the hospital] I came back, and I went to court.

And at this point how were you intending to plead? You hadn't pled in superior court.

No, I hadn't pleaded at all. I was just rapping, like I went to superior court once or twice. Three times. You know, the first two times I didn't plead at all; I just rapped.

About what?

About the finish, you know.

What kind of stuff did you talk about?

Well, the first time I went to court, [the judge] just told me,
Did I got a lawyer. I said no. I said, at that time, I wanted my
own lawyer, see. I didn't really want one, but again I was still delaying. So he said, You gonna get your own lawyer? I said yeah.
You know, in front of the judge I said I'd like to get my own
lawyer. So he said, We'll continue the case until tomorrow. So
I went back again the next day, and I think I told him the same
story; I'm not sure. Well, anyway, then I met Franklin. I was
rapping to him, and he said, It looks like you're not going to
have a public defender. I said I'm still working on getting [a
private attorney], you know. I said he's busy. You see, at first I
was going to have a lawyer by the name of—"DeAngelo." Now
DeAngelo was in the courtroom, but my mother hadn't notified
him. You see, I told him—my mother—I'm still delaying it.

*Wait, I'm not clear. Did you really want a private lawyer, or are
you just saying that so you could delay it?*

No, you see, I was pressing em for a deal, hoping that they
would say, Well, look, we gotta get this case; this case has been
continued so long let's get it over with. And then they come up
with a deal. So I went back to court the next day. [The judge]
says, We're going to appoint you public defender. So all right. I
didn't get to see him at all that day. I went back to jail. Then
I didn't hear any more when my court case gonna come up.

So the guy came to visit you in jail?

No.

The public defender?

No. So then I cut up again and went back to [the hospital] and
stayed about a month and a half; so altogether it was 112 days
before I went to court. Finally, the last day I went, and my
mother was there and everything; and my social worker, he was
talking; he came to see me. He said, If you plead guilty, we're
going to see if we can get it dropped down to a misdemeanor.
This means you get a year. You know, those two burglaries were
carrying a maximum of forty years; so I said it sounds all right.
Just what I wanted. So I went to court the next day—a couple
of days after I saw my social worker—and we rapped about it.
He says, All right? and I says yeah.

You're getting all this not directly from the public defender but through your social worker?

No, but what I'm saying now is that I went to court after I talked to my public defender, and I talked to him, I mean after I talked to my social worker. Then I talked to my public defender, Franklin. He said, "Yeah, well, I was talking to the district attorney, and he said he was going to see if he could get you your charges dropped down to misdemeanor." You know, if you cop out guilty. And so 90 percent of the time you cop out; he usually gets you what you want or what he offers you; so I says, Well, that sounds right.

You're going to cop out to both of them?

Right.

One of them you were innocent of?

Right. So then my mother was there and everything, and I went before the judge, and the judge, he asked me, Did I make any deals, you know. I said nah, no deals. He says, How you plead? I says guilty. So Franklin, he starts running off his mouth. He says, "Yeah, well ah, I file that we have the charges lessened to misdemeanor carrying a maximum of one year"; so public defender, I mean prosecutor, "Broussard," he went along with it; so the judge went along with it, and they sentenced me to a year in the state jail, and then they transferred me from the state jail up here.

Let me ask you a few questions. Where did you learn all these things about delay, they'll break it down, and this kind of stuff? Past experience?

No, well, I talk to a lot of people in jail, but *they* didn't delay it or anything like that. But, see, I knew Franklin, he didn't want to make this deal. You know, he wanted to hang me.

The public defender wanted to hang you?

Yeah, I think he wanted to hang me. So what I was doing, you know, I knew it was all over; the courts were flooded with all kinds of cases; so I guess they were disposing of them like mad; so they'd do anything just to get the case over with. So I delay them about three and a half months.

Are you telling me that you pled guilty to two, one which you did and one which you didn't?

Right.

How did you feel about pleading guilty to something that you didn't do?

Well, if I would've—he told me that if I would of went ahead with a jury trial, now they would of definitely hung me on one of them. Now, if I woulda went to the court and pleaded not guilty to one of them, asked for a jury trial on both the cases, they couldn't pay; they'd probably dismiss one of them, you see, but they'd hang me on the other one.

Did he tell you that?

Naw, but this is the way it works, you know what I mean. Like, let's say you have a whole lot of charges—aggravated assault, breach of peace. I had big charges. They'll drop all the big charges and leave you with the one little one and hang you on the little one. They'll give you the maximum time on the little one. You know what I mean? I figured this way: if I copped the both of them, I would of got a year; but if they would of hung me on the last one—in which they would have done cause I was caught dead in the act—I probably would have had an indefinite or a three-to-seven or a one-to-three—two-to-five, you know. Understand what I mean?

Yeah.

This is why I copped out.

Do you feel bitter about having to plead guilty to something you didn't do, or is it just the way it is?

That's the way; that's the name of the game. That's the game, you know, the game.

The prosecutor obviously let you off relatively easy and gave you a deal that was much less than you could have gotten.

Well, sure.

Why do you think they agreed to it?

Now you know a jury trial costs the state money, costs them quite a bit of money, and I was going to ask for jury of twelve, and I was going to go through a whole lot of hassle and cost the state a whole lot of money. So he figured we could avoid the state, like paying the jury—what, $150, $250—I don't know how much they're paying them—we gotta pay each jury, each guy on the jury, a sum of money, and it's costing the state, you see? This is why a guy, guys make this kind of deals, because the state don't want to pay all that money. They got like a little racket, the court racket. The public defender knows the prosecutor, you know; they drink together and play cards and———

Now, if you had it to do all over again, from the time you were arrested to the time you got sentenced, would you do anything different, or do you think you came out all right?

I would've done the same thing.

You think you did about as good as you could?

I think I made out like a bandit. I mean I had forty years hanging, the maximum. They could've gave me a ten-to-twenty on just one of them, cause twenty years is the maximum on burglary. They coulda gave me ten to twenty; they coulda gave me anything. They gave me twenty, nineteen, on the way down. Or they coulda gave me a one-to-two or two-to-five, but whatever he offers you, you better take it, cause if you don't, you're going to get more than he offered; so take what you get.

You came out pretty well?

Yeah, I mean from forty years down to one year, you know—good.

Both of these men pled guilty. Both expressed some reservations (though somewhat muted and perhaps ritualistic) about their actual guilt. One was quite dissatisfied with the outcome of his case; the other felt he "made out like a bandit." Both accepted bargains. Both distrusted their attorneys. Both in some ways felt that their adversary in the proceeding was not only the state and its representative, the prosecutor, but also their own attorney.

Let us explore more fully the stages through which the typical defendant passes on his way to sentencing day.

BAIL OR JAIL

A majority* of the defendants interviewed did not make bail and waited out their cases in pretrial detention. Although their recollections were sometimes fuzzy, it appears that the typical defendant spent at least a month in jail between arrest and final disposition. Failure to make bail resulted from a lack of money to pay the bail bondsman or a parole or probation violation "sticker"—a notation that the defendant was on parole or probation and hence was not eligible for bail because his probation or parole was likely to be revoked if he received another conviction.

The defendant in jail pending the outcome of his case is in a kind of limbo. He has been convicted of no crime but is detained, often in conditions much worse than those afforded to convicted criminals. He is isolated from his family and friends and from his attorney. He is not in a position to work to support his family nor to assist his attorney in the preparation of his defense. He is an object, shuttled back and forth from jail to court for numerous appearances that often amount to nothing.

Pretrial detention is often attacked as a violation of the presumption of innocence, for many are held for long periods of time without trial. The defendants interviewed greatly resented being held in jail. Their reasons, however, were not primarily those discussed above—their inability to continue to work and support their families or assist in their own defense. As suggested in the preceding chapter, most did not expect to beat their cases; most simply hoped for the best deal possible, a minimum sentence. They resented their stay in jail in part simply because of the terrible living conditions they encountered there and the lack of anything to do. "Unsentenced prisoners" (a somewhat ironic term, since they are presumed innocent) were typically not eligible to perform duties in the jails or participate in training or educational programs. They had to sit and wait, wondering what was going on outside and what was going to happen to them. They were isolated from their attorneys since most of their

---

* Thirty-eight of the seventy-one men interviewed did not make bail. Of the forty-nine men eventually sentenced to prison, only thirteen made bail; of the twenty-two men not sentenced to prison, twenty made bail.

public defenders did not visit the jails. They waited for their names to appear on the "court list" at night, were taken to the lock-up in the courthouse the next day, and perhaps had an opportunity to speak briefly with their public defender. They could receive visits from their immediate families, but usually a relative could not provide the information that was most desired: what was going to happen in the case.

In addition to the uncertainty and anxiety that pretrial detention involves, the defendants wanted to be on the streets simply to live: to walk around, shoot drugs, make love to a girl. On the streets, you don't have to *worry* as much. Finally, if the defendant is interested in and skilled at bargaining, he may wish to "wait them out"; but waiting them out on the streets is much easier than waiting them out in jail.

Thus, pretrial detention places great pressure upon the defendant. He feels a strong pressure to get it over with: to cop out and "escape" to prison—not only to free himself of the living conditions in jail, but also simply to reduce uncertainty. Once sentenced, he has something to shoot for: he knows his date of eligibility for parole. Before sentencing he knows nothing, or only that the future is unpleasant, but in a degree that is hard to anticipate.

Viewed from the perspective of maintaining the plea-bargaining system, pretrial detention and demoralizing conditions in jails are highly functional. They discourage the defendant from bargaining too hard; they place a high price upon filing motions or demanding a trial; they encourage him to rat out his friends in order to end his own ordeal. This is not to argue that those in authority consciously plan rotten jails; clearly most are concerned about jail conditions. But it is to suggest that such conditions are functional, do serve the needs of the production ethic that dominates our criminal justice system.

Pretrial detention can occasionally produce serious miscarriages of justice: men can be kept in jail for long periods of time and then be released without conviction. One man I spoke with spent nearly six months in jail before he was finally acquitted of a charge of robbery with violence. This case—and a few others I encountered in which charges were dismissed after a stay in jail—may be rare, but they are important. They are, in a sense, the "triumphs" of our legal system, for the innocent man is freed. But what lesson does the man learn? That the system is just? That, although mistakes are made, they are rectified? Hardly:

> When you messin with a dog, you got to be cool, because you got to watch out what he's gonna do.
>
> *The dog is the state?*
>
> The dog is the state, the cops, the judicial system. It's punishment before trial. I did six months—about 5½ months that I never get back in my life. How can they give me that back? They can't give it back!

The defendant who makes bail is in a much better position. He can continue to live his life, not completely obsessed by what kind of outcome his case will produce. If he wants to work, he can. If he wants to contact his attorney or public defender, he can do so. If he wants to resist a deal, he can, with some equanimity. If he wants to risk it all and go to trial, knowing that failure here will produce harsh punishment, he can do so without having to endure the six-to-nine-month delay that such a decision entails. Thus, whether he intends to cop out or to fight, he is simply in a better position to pursue his goals. He retains a kind of personal autonomy and sense of control over his destiny that jail takes from a man.

Which situation a man finds himself in—jail or out on bail—is largely a function of the nature of his charge (and hence the size of the bail), his past record, and the amount of money he possesses. The "justness" or "rationality" of these criteria may be debated, but it is clear that pretrial detention can affect both the outcome of his case and the quality of his life.[2]

FEAR OF THE TRIAL

Whether a defendant is in jail or out on bail, he has a number of alternatives available to him: he can maintain his innocence and demand a trial; he may engage in preliminary legal skirmishing, attempting, by way of a probable-cause hearing, motion to dismiss, or motion to suppress evidence, to attack the state's case and perhaps

obtain a dismissal or nolle;* he may simply cop out and accept whatever sentence is meted out; or he may bargain, threatening to go to
trial in an effort to obtain concessions on charges and sentence from
the prosecution.

Most defendants† chose one of the last two courses of action,
both involving pleas of guilty. Why didn't they exercise their right
to pretrial hearings and to their ultimate weapon, putting the state
to the test of sustaining its burden of proof at trial? The pretrial defendant might be expected to rely heavily on his attorney. His anxiety-
laden situation and the technical legal issues involved would seem to
require expert assistance for even the most sophisticated defendant.
In fact, the bulk of those interviewed—particularly if they were represented by public defenders—did not feel that they could trust their
attorneys.

We will discuss relationships between lawyer and client in detail
in the next chapter. At this point we may note that most defendants
saw their public defenders as both employees and in a real sense
agents of the state (the prosecution). Thus, their own attorney was
at best an indifferent middleman or broker attempting to mediate between defendant and prosecution and perhaps even a conscious agent
of the state. Thus, in making choices about what to do, the defendant
was the subject of advice from his attorney, but viewed such advice
with great suspicion. The lawyer was perceived, typically, as averse
to the exercise of legal rights, the filing of motions, and, especially, to
going to trial. If a defendant insisted, the attorney would of course
represent him at a trial, but he would do so only because he *had* to,
not because he wanted to.

> Well, when I went to court, I was supposed to go up for a jury
> trial that day. [The public defender] come out and asked me,
> blah blah blah, and I says, "Well, do you have any idea what
> the prosecutor has, as far as the information?" So he has a col-
> laborating witness, somebody that saw the sale of the gun take

---

* A prosecutor may simply decide not to proceed with a case against a
defendant. The charges are not formally dismissed, but the prosecutor grants a
nolle prosequi, indicating that the state does not at that time wish to proceed
with the case.

† Sixty-two of sixty-five defendants convicted in this sample; by most esti-
mates about 90 percent of all defendants found guilty in the United States.

place in front of the restaurant that my father was runnin and witnessed the whole thing. So I don't have much of a chance then, do I, as far as going through a jury trial? They're going to bury me.

Did he tell you what he thought you might get if you went to trial?

Well, he mentioned something about maybe six months to a year in jail or something like that, you know.

And you got the impression he figured they'd convict you?

Yeah, I got the impression that he was pretty sure that they might convict me.

Now, before this, did you have a feeling he wanted to go to trial? Do you think he cared one way or the other?

It didn't seem to me really that he cared that much. Not about going to trial in superior court—which in a way—the way the system is run, if you do go through trial and you're found guilty, why the hell should your sentence be heavier because you went through trial than it is if you plead guilty? You know? There should be no difference between that, but they more or less warn you if you put the court through the trouble of a trial by twelve jurors, and the expense of the court and everything, you're gonna pay for it if you're found guilty. They let you know that, and he sort of advised me to that fact, you know, and with my previous record—my history wasn't too good; so I didn't figure it would be too much; so I pled guilty to a lesser charge, substitute information—possession of stolen goods—he made a deal with me.

What was the deal?

Going to speak to the prosecutor about it and get six months suspended and two years probation. He went to the prosecutor, spoke to him, came back, guaranteed it—because you go before the judge; you don't say, I made a deal with the prosecutor, naturally. He says to you, "Have you been put under any duress as far as this substitute information or made any promises or anything like that?" And then the prosecutor made a recommendation as to sentence.

*   *   *

So what happened then?

So we picked the jury. After that we had a continuance, then we picked the jury.

How was your lawyer acting now?

He was still mad. He kept tellin me that I couldn't beat it; he says, Even if you are innocent, you're not gonna beat it; they find people that are innocent guilty, and you'll just end up with more time in jail; said I was facing a four-to-eight.

In these and most other cases, the public defender is offering quite rational advice, for there is substantial evidence against the defendant, and a trial will probably result in conviction. Thus, the advice and posture of the attorney is one factor contributing to the general fear of going to trial.

Another factor is mentioned by the first respondent quoted above: the assumption (which is probably quite correct) that if he goes to trial and is convicted, he will receive a harsher sentence than if he pleads guilty to the same offense. If he refuses to accommodate the state, he will be punished for his intransigence with a stiffer sentence. In a sense this is necessary for maintaining the plea-bargaining system, for it provides a crucial resource for the prosecutor. If the defendant had nothing to lose by going to trial (except the long wait that such a decision entails), he would have less incentive to agree to the deal.

A final factor contributing to the fear of trial is the belief that if there is a conflict of testimony, the state's witnesses, especially if they are police officers, will be believed. The defendants feel that they— and their friends—do not enjoy the credibility that state's witnesses possess. Thus, if the outcome of the case rests upon two accounts of an event—theirs and the state's—the state will prevail.

They got to take the police's word, you know what I mean?

Why do they have to?

Because he's superior.

They think he's superior?

He is superior. He is. He is superior.

How?

Oh, I mean, now I can be walking down the street, anybody walking down this street, you know what I mean? If a cop come here and punch you in the head with a stick, you know what I mean? Only thing he can say was, "He tried to hit me first." And they gonna say, "Oh, you did this?" And you say, "Naw, I'm not guilty, this man's lying." [They say] "I'm sorry, I have to go with this report here."

This is what the judge says?

This is what the judge'll say.

You think the judges just sort of instinctively believe what the cops tell them?

They're gonna believe it.

Why?

Because the judge, they like brothers. A brother's gonna stick up for his brother.

All these are reasonably rational calculations and are usually correct. But it is crucial to understand the power of such factors. Even the man who righteously maintains his innocence may submit to a guilty plea because of his fear of trial. Even the man who has an attorney who wants to fight may give in.

The following defendant was one of the few with whom I spoke who had been convicted and protested his innocence. His case, which was highly publicized, involved two charges: second-degree murder in the slaying of a police undercover agent and a charge of breaking and entering that had been pending for about a year before the killing of the police officer. The defendant was represented by two attorneys—a private attorney in the murder case and a legal service office attorney in the B and E. He claimed that the shooting of the police officer was in self-defense (and had several witnesses willing to testify to this) and that the B and E had occurred while he was sleeping in the car of friends who had committed the break. At the point at which we pick up his account, the prosecutor had offered to drop the murder charge to manslaughter:

So August fourth I went to court. [My lawyers] were both in court, and they came downstairs. They said the State's Attorney wanted me to cop out to nine to eighteen years for everything— B and E, possession of burglary tools, and manslaughter. So I said, "Well, I can't do that, you know." [My lawyer] said, "I told them that you wasn't going for it." He said, "But since they told me to tell you, I came here to tell you." So he went back upstairs; about an hour later he come back and he said they were down to 5½ to 9. So I said, "No." He went back up there; about another half-hour he come back, and he said that they were down to 3½ to 5. I said, "Well, you go back up there now; see if they go for a suspended sentence." I said, "I cop out for a suspended sentence." So he went back upstairs, and he didn't come back. So that afternoon I went upstairs, and he had some motions, he'd filed some motions. He filed a lot of motions, and the judge granted a couple of them. Then he brought the jury panel in.

So now you're about ready to go to trial?

Yeah. So then they brought in a jury panel, about thirty-five people, all of em, I'd say, mostly old people, about fifty to seventy years old. Some of 'em they had to hold 'em up to bring em in, you know. So they brought all these old people in and asked them a few questions, and I just didn't feel like—out of those people, you know—I didn't feel like I was going to get a jury of my peers and they didn't care one way or the other what happened. So my sister and my girlfriend, they was scared. Of course they didn't want me getting all that time, you know, so they said, "Take the three-to-five, and go and get on and do that time because if you get convicted and they give you a life sentence, you might get out on appeal, but it gonna take a lot of time." So I said OK.

The defendant later related a story of another case he had observed while waiting in court:

So, in this guy's case, they got up there and said that this guy sell a police informer some dope, and the guy was cleanshaven, and he was standing three feet from the witness. So this guy's lawyer subpoenaed the police mug shot. They brought that over, and this guy got a beard down to here [laughs]; he got a beard that long. So they showed it to the jury, and then they put this cop back on the stand. He said, "Well, by the man being black-skinned, I might have made a mistake about him being clean-shaven." So the judge told the jury, "A case of mistaken identity and circumstantial evidence." And they went in and stayed about fifteen minutes and then found him guilty. So, man, here I go up there, and I'm admitting to shooting this man. And when that's all they want, you know. I felt like that's all they wanted to hear—you shot him. How it happened don't make no dif-ference; you shot him, you get it? And I don't feel like, in other words, I don't want to start serving no life sentence that way.

The defendant's private attorney wanted to go to trial:

> *What about your lawyer? Had he said anything to you about what he thought you ought to do?*
>
> Yeah, he said he wanted to fight. He asked me whether I was satisfied with the deal, and I said that I wasn't satisfied with it, but I felt that I made the best choice, you know. And he said long as I felt that way, he was OK, he said. But I blew his chance of him winning his first murder case. He actually wanted to fight it, and I had a lot of confidence in him.

As the defendant stressed repeatedly, When's the last time you have heard of a man who kills a cop and gets a 3½-year sentence? What-ever the truth is, the story he tells indicates that even a man who righteously maintains his innocence (much less the self-admittedly guilty man who might have some potential legal defense) may dis-trust the jury system, may be unwilling to believe that he will be taken seriously, that he has a reasonable chance of acquittal.

Thus, most may threaten a trial but are in reality afraid of having one. For most this is a perfectly rational fear, for they are in fact guilty, and the state could probably bear its burden of proof and convict them should they go to trial. Most of the men who cop out are, thus, probably acting in their own interest. Among the men I spoke with who were convicted, only three of sixty-five actually went to trial. One was acquitted (but, as discussed above, spent nearly six months in jail waiting for trial); the other two asserted their innocence but were convicted. Their decision to go to trial was in part the product of extreme alienation: a hatred for the police and the courts and a desire to exact a price from them:

You figured you'd probably get convicted?

I knowed it.

Did they offer you a deal if you'd cop out?

Yeah, he [the special public defender representing this defendant] told me he could get me a deal—eighteen months to three, stuff like that, yeah.

What did he tell you you would likely get if you went to trial?

He say, "You know you get a lot bigger sentence." I told him that wasn't the point about the bigger sentence, it wasn't the point about that. I says, "The point is that I was not guilty." If I was guilty, I would go and tell em I was guilty and plead guilty. I said the point is *where* I lose the war. I said, "It's gonna cost them some money." I say people haven't challenged these people and know what's bein done up on the table.

Well, why didn't you take the deal?

Well, I didn't take it, no, shit no. I wasn't guilty; I wasn't taking nothin like that. Say, I'm not one of them and they can give me a piece of candy and tell me go on out there and go to play. I'm not that type of guy, and they knows it. See, they just can't give me anything. They told me, "Well, we don't put ourselves out for a man like you." I said, "Well, I'll show them and my people that they had a black man that you could be proud of, that fight his case."

If you had it to do over again, would you do it the same way?

I would—I would do it a little worser.

How's that?

Every time I go, every time I go through the courts, I learns a little bit more and more about law. I learns how much game they play on a man—that's all a politician is, is games.

This man was convicted at a jury trial of aggravated assault, on the basis of testimony by three witnesses that he had fired a gun at another man. His discussion of the facts of his case was somewhat vague and often evasive. Perhaps he was innocent, perhaps not. The point is that he was at the same time a "principled" man who was not going to take any more "shit" from the system, and a deeply embittered man who went to trial and received a 3½-to-5-year sentence instead of the 1½ to 3 years that he had been offered, as a token of his contempt for the system.

The other defendant who went to trial and was convicted was charged with aggravated assault arising from a struggle with police officers. He maintained his innocence, asserting that he was only defending himself. His conviction after trial resulted in a two-to-five-year sentence in the reformatory and taught him a lesson about what to do in the future:

> I'd just get a public defender and cop out [laughs]. If the charges ain't nothin like murder—if this is another charge like this, I'd just cop out and get less time, mister, because I see that I can't win, because I might be guilty next time.

Thus, most men avoid the backbone of our system of justice—the trial. The reasons for this decision—their lawyers' perceived reluctance, the harsher punishment they face, their lack of credibility—are often the product of rational calculation.

The lack of trials reduces the significance of the procedural guarantees that our system putatively offers to defendants. Many of these guarantees—for example, protections against coercive station-house interrogation, unreasonable searches and seizures, and entrapment—are largely enforceable through trial. That is, the sanctioning mechanism that is supposed to prevent such police abuses involves the assertion by the defendant that his rights have been violated and the exclusion of evidence illegally obtained. Defendants, by refusing to go to trial, sacrifice their right to exercise such defenses. In particular cases this may mean that persons who are not "legally" guilty—whose guilt cannot be proved, given the constraints supposedly imposed on police conduct—are in fact convicted, with their own tacit or explicit consent. In more general terms, the lack of trials means that the procedural rules enunciated by courts—especially in recent years the Supreme Court—are not the serious concern that they would be for police officers if the latter had the expectation that all or most defendants would challenge illegal police practices.

Moreover, the fear of trials undermines the very nature of the system of presumption of innocence and burden of proof on the state. For, from the defendant's eyes, he is presumed not innocent but guilty. He must prove his innocence. Given the difficulties that he sees in doing so, he usually will not try. This reduces his respect for the system as a whole, for it suggests hypocrisy. As one man quoted above suggested: why should a man who goes to trial be punished more heavily than one who cops out? In terms of the impact upon the defendant, the penalty exacted for going to trial may not be such a good thing. In the short run, it offers an advantage to the man who cops out, for he gets off more lightly than he might. In the long run, it reinforces the lesson that the system operates not on the basis of principles of morality or legality, but on the basis of resources and their exploitation.

It may be objected here and at other points that I am employing a dual standard, asking the "system" to live up to certain principles in its treatment of defendants while apparently being tolerant of their own often harmful and destructive behavior. As I argue at various points below, I think the system *ought* to be "better" than the defendants. If the criminal justice system is to have the capacity to help those who go through it, the capacity to enable them to emerge from their encounter with less likelihood of engaging in criminal acts in the future, it must not simply mirror their own lives. If it is to teach lessons, it must in part teach them by example.

BARGAINING AND THE PLEA OF GUILTY

After the defendant has been arrested, arraigned, and bond has been set, the stage is set for the crucial activity of the criminal justice system: plea-bargaining. It is, in many ways, a game. There are at least two, perhaps three, "sides," and each possesses resources and goals. The outcome depends largely upon the vigor and skill with which each side exploits its resources.

The vagueness about the number of teams indicates the somewhat anomalous role played by the defendant's attorney. The two obvious sides are the defendant and the prosecution.* The lawyer is clearly also a crucial participant, but his side in the game is often unclear. In general, if he is a private retained attorney, he is perceived by the defendant as being on his side; if he is a public defender, he is viewed as a member of the prosecutor's team, or sometimes as a middleman or broker. The sources of these perceptions are discussed in detail in the next chapter. Here, we will focus primarily upon the defendant's view of the nature of the game.

Most defendants view the game as one that they cannot, in an absolute sense, "win." It is a game in which they can, should they choose to play and be skillful or lucky, lose less than they would if they failed to play at all. To some extent their ability to play depends upon the prosecutor's willingness to bargain: if the prosecutor refuses to bargain but simply makes an offer and will not budge, then the defendant does not actively bargain; he either acquiesces or goes to trial. This unwillingness appears to occur relatively infrequently. It is most likely to occur when there is strong pressure upon the prosecution to obtain maximum sentences for a particular class of crime: for example, after a notorious case of child rape, the prosecutor may refuse to bargain, for a time, with those charged with sex offenses involving children; after a series of highly publicized drug arrests allegedly involving dealers or pushers, the prosecution may be unwilling, for a time, to engage in reduction of charges from sales to possession, usually a common form of bargain.

But in most cases the defendant will, at some point, be offered a deal—some charge reduction, sentence agreement, or both, in return for a plea of guilty. The prosecutor holds most of the cards in the plea-bargaining game—at least as most defendants see it, for he is viewed as having the power to determine the sentence. Although technically he can only make a recommendation to the judge, his recommendations are usually followed. Occasionally a judge may intervene and impose a higher or lower sentence than is recommended, but usually he will go along. Most defendants believed that the judge is a hidden partner to the agreement; and in many cases the prosecutor does clear the deal with the judge before committing himself to it. Thus, the prosecutor determines the fate of the case: he can dismiss

---

* In some jurisdictions, there is another player—the judge; in Connecticut, judges do not play particularly obvious roles in plea-bargaining.

or nolle some or all charges; he can agree to a suspended sentence; he can determine the number of years that the defendant must spend in jail or prison.

Although he is viewed as having this power, he is also perceived to have goals that affect his discretion in its exercise. His major goal, from the defendants' perspective, is to get convictions and turn cases over as quickly as possible. Like the police officer, the prosecutor is viewed as a worker, and his job places constraints upon what he is likely to do in a case. He does not want to go to trial, because this takes time and money.* The prosecutor is not viewed as particularly interested in the characteristics of any given defendant or case. The defendants believe that factors such as background, motive, and treatment needs are not particularly important in the prosecutor's decisions about what concessions to make. This lack of concern stems, they believe, not from the prosecutor's conscious malevolence, but from the nature of his job. As with their attitude toward policemen, defendants can both resent and sympathize with such behavior.

What resources do defendants possess? The list of potential resources includes money, status, and the credibility that they produce; the ability to demand a trial; fortitude in "waiting them out"; and, often, luck. Most defendants did not possess either of the first two resources in quantities that were of any use. Most could not even afford to hire their own attorney, much less engage investigative resources or make the payoffs that they believe are crucial to success in the legal system. "Money talks" in their view, and any defendant with sufficient resources can buy his way out of almost any trouble. This view was almost unanimous among the men with whom I spoke. When a man mentioned payoffs, he was asked whether he knew of any instance in which this had occurred. A few asserted that they did; the majority simply accepted the premise that everyone has his price. Some defendants were more sophisticated about the power of money: it enables a defendant to make bail and hence wait out the prosecution more effectively; it enables him to hire a good attorney, who will —because he is being paid well—exercise himself vigorously on behalf

---

* This is clearly a correct perception; the only striking distortion in defendants' perception was that they tended to think that what the prosecutor wanted to avoid was literally the cost of paying the jurors in a trial, rather than the expense in time and manpower of the prosecutor's staff that trials entail.

of his clients. Finally, money, in our society, brings the status which is crucial to one's credibility, both as a witness and in making representations to prosecutors and judges about future good conduct. Thus, in the defendants' view the crucial resource in the bargaining game is "the big scratch," a resource which they regrettably do not have in great supply.

Defendants lack money and status, but they are not without resources. They still have the ability to demand a trial and to wait "them" out. Demanding a trial is really a bluffer's game: it is a threat and a bargaining counter, but most would be loath to actually go to trial. Thus, the defendant must exploit this resource with great care. He can continue to turn down offers and enter a plea of not guilty and have a trial date set. He may—as two of the men quoted above indicated—get as far as jury selection and perhaps some testimony at his trial. But he wants to avoid having the jury bring in a verdict. Pursuing a strategy of "waiting them out," the defendant can simply refuse offers made to him and have his court appearance continued until a satisfactory deal is offered. The majority of the men interviewed did not have this kind of fortitude. They usually reported rejecting a single offer and then accepting the second one made, which sometimes was identical with the first. Even this strategy sometimes involved fairly long waits, for continuances are often for two weeks, and rejecting an offer could mean a month's delay waiting in jail.

Eventually, whether it took three weeks or three months, the majority of defendants did make a deal and agree to plead guilty. It is crucial to notice that the deal determines the penalty that the offender must pay for his crime. Thus, the decision about what punishment (and "rehabilitation") the defendant receives is not, from his view at least, determined on the basis of characteristics that seem relevant to such a decision: his motives for committing the crime, the nature of the offense and the harm done, his personal history and needs. Rather, it is the product of a kind of game, in which he possesses quite limited resources. Whether he plays the game skillfully and loses less than he might, or whether he plays diffidently or not at all, the outcome is still a matter of the application of resources and power. The prosecutor may, in fact, take account of these individualistic factors in making offers, but the defendants do not see it that way. The deal seems largely determined by systemic factors: how crowded the courts are, whether court officials are highly concerned about a certain kind of crime, personal contacts, or the intervention of luck—the judge or prosecutor had seen a defendant play basketball, or they had misspelled a defendant's name and didn't have his arrest record and realize how extensive it was.

The situation the defendant faces in the period preceding his eventual plea is, in many respects, an extension of his life in the streets. You scuffle around, trying to accumulate a little wealth or power; you con others and are conned by them; you exploit those you can and are exploited by those who are more powerful; you use people for your own ends and are, in turn, used by others. You lie, you cheat, you care little about abstract moral principles. How you make out on the street depends upon what you've got and how you use it. In addition, luck and fate are crucial elements of life in the streets. Often the events that occur are accidental: you come into some money easily; you get burned and lose it. You are to a large extent at the mercy of others and of fate. You try to get what you want, but whether you get it or not often has little to do with your efforts.

These same characteristics seem to the defendants to characterize their experience within the legal system. Their initial arrest is often simply the product of bad luck: they are arrested for an activity that they have been engaging in frequently. Something goes wrong, and they get caught. They then must attempt to make the best of their situation and use the techniques that they already know well in order to attempt to ameliorate their plight. The other participants in the system seem to be doing the same things. They are going about their jobs in fashions that seem to the defendants quite similar to the hypocritical and manipulative ways in which they themselves treat people. And they are probably correct. The attention and care that is paid to the "criminal" after his arrest is quite similar to the attention and care that our society generally pays to its poor and its black; so his belief in the similarity of court and street life is by no means unrealistic.

THE COP-OUT CEREMONY

The peculiar and somewhat hypocritical nature of a system which is based upon the presumption of innocence, due process values, and the criminal trial, but which in practice is a game of plea-bargaining, is reinforced by what is known as the cop-out ceremony. After a defendant has agreed to plead guilty, he appears before a judge to enter his plea. He is asked a series of questions about whether he is pleading guilty because he is in fact guilty, about coercion or inducements to plead, about his satisfaction with the representation afforded him by his attorney. The purposes of going through this litany are somewhat murky. Ostensibly, the questions are designed to make sure that defendants are not pleading guilty (as a result of coercion, extravagant promises, and so forth) to things they did not do. As suggested above, most are pleading guilty in return for some kind of promise, and some even maintain their innocence yet still plead guilty. In recognition of the operation of the plea-bargaining system, the Supreme Court recently held, in *North Carolina* v. *Alford*,[3] that a guilty plea may be accepted from a man who maintains his innocence as long as there is evidence of guilt and the plea is made voluntarily. In the *Alford* case, a man pled guilty to second-degree murder, although he maintained that he was innocent. His attorney advised him to plead guilty to avoid the possible death penalty that might result from a first-degree murder conviction at trial. There was substantial circumstantial evidence against the defendant. The *Alford* decision recognizes the plea-bargaining system, acknowledging that a man may maintain his innocence but still plead guilty in order to minimize his potential loss. By requiring that there be some evidence of guilt in such a situation, the decision attempts to protect the "really" innocent from the temptations to which plea-bargaining and defense attorneys may subject them.

In addition to presumably assuring that innocent men are not being forced or induced to plead guilty by extravagant promises, the questioning of the defendant entering a guilty plea serves other, latent functions. Some have called it a "successful degradation ceremony" in which a defendant is forced to shed publicly his identity as innocent citizen and accept the identity of "criminal." [4] Another view of the process, suggested by Abraham Blumberg, is as follows:

> The "cop-out" ceremony is invaluable as a formally structured ritual for the benefit of significant *organizational* "others." The accused not only is made to assert publicly his guilt of a specific

crime but to recite completely its details. He must further indicate that he is entering his plea of guilty freely, willingly, and voluntarily; and that he is not doing so because of any promises or in consideration of any commitments which anyone may have made to him. This last is intended as a blanket statement to shield the participants from any possible charges of coercion or undue influence in violation of due process requirements. Its function is to preclude any later review by an appellate court on these grounds and similarly to obviate any second thoughts an accused may develop about his plea. The "cop-out" is in fact a charade, during which an accused must project an appropriate and acceptable degree of guilt, penitence, and remorse. If he adequately feigns the role of the "guilty person," his hearers will engage in the fantasy that he is contrite and thereby merits a lesser plea. One of the essential functions of the criminal lawyer is that he coach his accused client in this performance. What is involved, therefore, is not a "degradation" or "reinforcing" process at all, but rather a highly structured system of exchange cloaked in the rituals of legalism and public professions of guilt and repentance. Everyone present is aware of the staging, including the defendant.[5]

Most of the men I spoke with did in fact see the cop-out ceremony as a charade:

Well, they say that when you come before him [the judge] in court, has any deals been made?

He asked you that?

Yes.

And you said?

No.

Now, do you think he knew you were lying [the respondent had previously described the deal made in his case]?

He knew I'm lying; he knew the deal was made; he knew good and well I was lying.

Why do you think he asked you the question then?

Why? Because some people have been trying to get their cases back in court because they've been double-crossed.

So this is to cover themselves?

That's right, that's right. That's all, just a shield. Yeah, that's justice.

*   *   *

Think back to the time you went before the judge to change your plea to guilty and you pled guilty to attempted B and E. Did the judge ask you any questions?

Yeah [laughs].

Did your lawyer tell you how to answer them beforehand?

No, but you know how to answer them. He [the judge] asked me, you know, like had you ever been—you haven't been offered any kind of deal or nothing. He didn't put in that word, but it was meant the same thing. You have to say "No." If anybody's in the courtroom, you gotta make a little show for them.

What do you think the point of it is?

That's a hard one. I don't know really. That's just like everything. There got to be a cover; you got to cover up.

Who are they covering it up from? The public?

Yeah.

How do you think people would react if they knew there were deals?

They would react the same way they found out that Nixon had him a girlfriend on the sideline.

You mean they'd think it was wrong?

Yeah, they would bitch about it. I take that back; but they might have a big writeup; they probably have a thing in the magazine, something in the newspapers, and they want the government to look into it, and they want the mayor to look into it; and the mayor, he, the people who vote, you know, the governor needs votes, he don't want that shit coming off.

You think people wouldn't like it if they found out that everything was done by deals?

I don't think so; I don't think most people would like it, cause that's making the American way of life sort of, like, the justice, the freedom, you can pull yourself up, the Abraham Lincoln thing, where you can come from a log cabin to the president, the White House, you know . . . they fucked all that up, you know.

Thus, the defendant must appear before the judge and go through a ritual. The judge asks him questions, and he responds with lies; the judge knows they are lies and accepts his answer as true. Once more the defendant is placed in a position in which he must play out a game. Some of them have a good idea what the game is about: to prevent a double cross by a defendant; to make things look right to the public. Others don't understand its purpose at all: when asked why they thought they had to answer the questions, they responded with confusion; it was just something you had to do, and probably "they" (the judges, the prosecutor, the state) had a reason for it, but the reason wasn't clear.

From the defendant's perspective, it did not seem to be a particularly demeaning or degrading experience. They did not really "shed" one identity and assume another—at least in their own eyes. They were the same before and after: they were criminals. Blumberg seems right when he speaks of it as a kind of exchange. The recognition that there is some kind of exchange emerged when defendants were asked what they thought might happen if they had not acted their part properly; for example, had they responded that they had made a deal, or had they denied their guilt.

No, he [the judge] probably would have said, "Well, I think your lawyer got to consult with you," you know.

* * *

Both the prosecutor and the defending attorney would have denied any knowledge of any such deal and figured I was making the whole thing up—trying to make the court look bad. And the judge would have taken that into consideration when he gave me a sentence.

But the defendant doesn't see himself as giving up anything of great value: he is simply speaking words, and they don't seem to mean very much.

In the cop-out ceremony, the defendant again faces a game and a situation that vividly pits the "theory" of the system against its reality. Certain forms must be gone through which indicate concern with him as a person: *he* must get up there and answer questions; the questions are directed at him and at his behavior and attitudes (Did he do it? Is he satisfied with his counsel?). But once again the individual attention seems largely a sham, a ritual to be gotten over rather than something with real meaning. Their attorney instructs them how to answer the questions, or they simply know that they must do it in a certain fashion. What appears to unsophisticated observers as an individualized act is to the defendant (and to the attorney, the prosecutor, and probably many judges) simply a charade. This same aura surrounds the defendant's other major appearance before the judge: sentencing.

SENTENCING

The second crucial appearance before a judge occurs when the defendant appears for sentencing. In the typical case in Connecticut, after a defendant is found guilty (either by plea or after a trial), a two-week continuance is granted by the judge for a presentence investigation. This investigation, conducted by members of the probation office, results in the Presentence Report, which is available to the prosecutor and judge and, typically, to public defenders and defense attorneys who are on good terms with the prosecutor's office. The report is a fairly lengthy document based upon police reports, arrest records, and interviews with the defendant and often a few of his relatives. The report presents a description of the offense based upon police reports, a section entitled "Offender's Version," a fairly detailed description of the defendant's background (educational, occupational, family history, and past arrests and convictions), and occasionally a recommendation about whether the defendant ought to be incarcerated. Although the reports deal largely with the objective "facts" of a defendant's life and not with his psychological characteristics or internal dynamics, information is available to those who must pass judgment upon him.

On sentencing day the prosecutor, the defense attorney, and the defendant himself are permitted to speak, although most defendants do not do so. The prosecutor speaks about the defendant's crime, his background and past history, and typically makes a recommendation to the judge about what sentence he ought to receive. The defense attorney also speaks, noting facts about the defendant that he feels are relevant in determining sentence. The judge then passes sentence upon the defendant. Perceptions of the judge are discussed in detail in Chapter 5. Here we may note that he is viewed as essentially a figurehead: he gives what the prosecutor recommends and thus possesses a stamp which can legitimate the deal. He does not, in the defendant's eyes, usually exercise independent authority. "The prosecutor is the man who gives the time," is the standard refrain of defendants, and they are probably largely right.

Although sentencing day is naturally an occasion for some anxiety, for most defendants the outcome is not unexpected. They have copped out in return for an agreement about sentence and usually receive what they have agreed to. The major anxiety for most—and it is not a really nagging concern—is the possibility of a double cross. The prosecutor may double-cross them and recommend more time than had been promised;* the judge may double-cross them and give more than the prosecutor recommends; their attorney may double-cross them and not recommend a drug program when he has said he will. Usually none of these occurs, and the defendant is sentenced—on recommendation of the prosecutor—to the punishment to which he has agreed.

For a few defendants sentencing day was one of real anxiety. These defendants had not arrived at an agreement about sentence. In these relatively few cases either their attorney had not told them of an agreement (which seemed more characteristic of private attorneys than of public defenders) or an agreement had not been reached. This latter situation, as suggested before, typically occurred when the crime was one which is the subject of either publicity or particular concern by the prosecution. In such a situation defendants may plead guilty anyway: the state has a strong case against them, and their attorney advises that they had better plead guilty and see what will

---

* A recent Supreme Court decision has held that the prosecutor is obligated to recommend the sentence agreed to in a plea-bargain, though the judge is not legally bound to accept the recommendation. See *Santobello* v. *New York*, 404 U.S. 257 (1971).

happen rather than go to trial. In such situations the prosecution may or may not make a recommendation to the judge in open court. In either case, when the defendant appeared for sentencing, he did not know what he would get. He knew the maximum he faced, but not what the judge would actually impose.

Whether there is a deal or not, the defendant does not feel that the sentence he receives is the product of attention to him as an individual. If he has agreed to a deal, the defendant will likely get it, but not because the judge or prosecutor has decided that the particular sentence is in any sense "best" for him, but rather because this is what induced him to plead guilty and get it over with. If there is no deal, again this is typically perceived as the product of extraneous factors: publicity, fear of a certain offense. The defendant in this situation may be "made an example of" in response to public pressure, but, again, this has little to do with *him*.

The defendants believe that the deal that they receive depends mainly upon their past record: a man can expect to receive an offer that varies directly with his past record. The more convictions he has, the more time he will have to serve for his current offense. The defendants are somewhat ambivalent about this fact. On the one hand, they resent it, for they are inclined to believe that it constitutes a kind of multiple jeopardy in which they continue to pay for what they did in the past. On the other hand, when asked directly, they admit that if they were judges or prosecutors, they would behave in similar fashion: punish more heavily those who were repeated offenders than those who were there for the first time. Thus, when asked how a judge decides what sentence to give a man, the majority responded that he went by what the prosecutor said. When asked how the prosecutor decided, they stressed their past records and his need to get the case over with.

Did the men think that they had been sentenced fairly? In general the answer is yes. Clearly, any such generalization must be made with care. None of the men I spoke with wanted to be in prison or on probation. Most would, not unnaturally, have desired lesser sentences than they received. A few were quite bitter about their sentences, feeling that they had been double-crossed by the prosecutor or their attorney, that codefendants should not have received lesser sentences, or that they should be in drug programs rather than in prison.

But most of the men were not bitter about their sentences. Many were uncomfortable and confused in considering the question, "Do you think your sentence was fair?" Fairness is a concept which is not —except in an often somewhat hollow and even wistful fashion— especially salient to the men with whom I spoke. Although a few had real concern about abstract concepts such as fairness or justice, most were concerned with the world as it is rather than as it might be. Thus, "fairness" was measured not against some abstract notion about what is just (e.g., "the punishment fits the crime" or "equal punishment for crimes causing equal harm") but rather against reality. Thus, a "fair" sentence meant largely two things to the men: (1) a good deal—something less than they might have gotten; (2) the going rate for an offense. Neither of these has a great deal to do with notions of rehabilitation or individual treatment, with notions of what is just punishment for the offense which a man committed, taking into account such things as the nature of the offense, the amount of harm done, motive, alternative modes of treatment, past activity. Perhaps these are implicit in their notions, but basically they view the concept of "fairness" in sentencing as either getting off light, or at least not getting above the going rate.

Listen to a few of their remarks:

Do you think the sentence you received was fair?

Yes, yes, definitely. Now, robbery with violence and plus motor vehicle, I'd probably be doin more time—now I know I'd be doing more time. So I think I got an even break—by they giving me this, you know, one to two. So I kind of got even break on me.*

*   *   *

Do you think the sentence you received was fair?

Not really.

* A charge against this defendant of robbery with violence was nollied, and he was sentenced only for taking a motor vehicle.

Suppose you'd been a judge and someone had come before you for sentencing and had all your characteristics—pled guilty to these two counts, what would you have given him?

Well, then again in a way I think I might have gave him almost the same because the fact is, he did plead guilty; and, like I say, they can't get in, they don't get into the cases, and they really don't read what they—I mean, just by reading some of them reports, you can't tell whether a man is guilty or not guilty.

Well, you say you were guilty of one of the charges but not the other.

Hmmm. And, well, they didn't really care long as the, you know, they just wanted to more or less get rid of the case.

*   *   *

Do you think it was a fair sentence?

Yeah, it was all right.

Now, suppose you'd been a judge and a guy came before you who was you. Had everything good about you, everything bad about you. Had all your characteristics and had pled guilty on a possession charge, what would you have sentenced him to?

Well, I don't know what I would have sentenced him to. I would go by what the prosecutor was ready to.

The way you described what happened, you pled guilty to something you say you didn't do. How do you feel about it?

How do I feel?

You don't seem especially bitter about it.

No, I don't. You know, my main concern was being on the street.* I don't give a shit how I had to do it, what procedure was to do it, just be there. Not locked up. Because I don't, I can't stand being locked up and taking orders from people. You know, I'm very independent within myself; so the changes I had to go through—if I have to lie, it doesn't make me no difference. As long as I'm on the street. I'm not locked up.

*   *   *

* The defendant received a suspended sentence.

Do you think it was a fair sentence?

Like I said, I'm a little prejudiced about myself. I think I did
pretty good [laughs].

*   *   *

Do you think it was a fair sentence?

I don't know; I can't really say.

*Suppose you were a judge and a guy came before you with all
your characteristics; you know, pled guilty to two B and E's,
everything good about you, everything bad about you—what
do you think you would have given him?*

I don't know. Most likely I probably give him the same sentence
he gave me. I don't know, because all judges are different. Maybe
the judge, like, a lot of peoples don't look at it this way, like
the judge may come, he might have a bad day today, or he might
not feel right, you know what I mean, and maybe he don't want
to hear this case, and he just say, Well, indefinite term in
Cheshire reformatory; and that's all he says, and he just go back
home, until another case.

*So you think the judge doesn't care about what happens to a
guy? Why is that? Is it the kind of man that's a judge, or the job
makes a man, or? . . .*

Really he can't, you know what I mean?

Why not?

Because maybe sixty dudes go in front of the judge that day,
right? just say for instance. Now, he can't remember all sixty
of those, because look at all the hundreds, or maybe perhaps
thousands, that he had before he got this sixty. So it's impossible
for him to really care, unless maybe somethin that really happened, or somethin that is tragic, made him to remember what
had happened. But if I were to come up to that judge, when I
get out if I would go up to him and say, "Do you remember
me?" he don't even know me. And again maybe if he looked at
his record, he probably could remember what had happened. So
that shows right there that he couldn't possibly care. So there's
no way that I can see that a judge care about me. After I leave
the courtroom, it's all forgotten. But, see, it's on record.

Thus, in general the men were not dissatisfied with their sentences. Most wished they had received less time. Many addicts felt that they would be better off in a hospital than in prison. A few felt that they had suffered real injustice—particularly the men who had received very stiff terms and who had little previous experience with the criminal justice system. Some suggested that characteristics such as motive or background should have played a greater role in sentencing.

They tended to measure their sentences against what they *might* have received rather than against what was good for them in an abstract fashion. Once more, this is something that a man is likely to learn from his contact with the system. There is such a thing as a going rate; the system does produce some regularity in sentencing, with a defendant's prior record the major determinant of his sentence. The men know this and accept it—for they *must* accept it. Hence, they are resigned and don't see the point in theorizing about what might be. Fair is a good break or a reasonable sentence; unfair is too much time, time beyond the going rate.

To say that the men emerge in general not bitterly dissatisfied is not to say that the system is working properly. One does not need to introduce any particularly sophisticated "false consciousness" argument to suggest that resignation is not necessarily the end product that the system ought to produce. Most of the men are aware that something other than a going rate ought to determine a man's sentence. That they accept the fact that *they* can't do anything about this and so resign themselves to their treatment is not to say that their basic needs have been fulfilled or that everything is all right. Once more, the lessons of the criminal justice system are quite different from the lessons we might wish to be teaching defendants.

JUSTIFICATIONS FOR THE PLEA-BARGAINING SYSTEM

These views of the nature of American justice are not simply the fantasies of men who got in trouble. They accurately represent the observations of many judges, prosecutors, defense counsel, and scholars who have examined the nature of American justice. Why do we have a system of "bargain justice"? What functions does it serve? Are there arguments to be made in its favor?

A variety of justifications for the plea-bargaining system have been offered. One of them—the sheer volume of cases facing the courts— looms above all others. Many of the other arguments have a kind of *post hoc* character—they appear to have been formulated in order to justify a situation which is too difficult to remedy. The need for turning cases over is illustrated by the following remarks of a judge, made in 1937, but perhaps even more apposite today:

> Let us suppose that five hundred cases are on the list for trial at a sitting of court. Of these, one hundred cases are tried, and four hundred defendants plead guilty. Seldom is there time in a sitting to try more than a fifth of the cases on the list. . . . The prosecutor must subordinate almost everything to the paramount need of disposing of his list during the sitting. Rather than dismiss the excess by nolle prosequi, with no penalty, he must induce defendants in fact guilty to plead guilty, in order that some penalty may be imposed. Half a loaf is better than no bread.
>
> If all the defendants should combine to refuse to plead guilty, and should dare to hold out, they could break down the administration of criminal justice in any state in the Union. But they dare not hold out, for such as were tried and convicted could hope for no leniency. The prosecutor is like a man armed with a revolver who is cornered by a mob. A concerted rush would overwhelm him. . . . The truth is that a criminal court can only operate by inducing the great mass of actually guilty defendants to plead guilty.[6]

In addition to administrative considerations, other quite cogent arguments for plea-bargaining have been advanced. One suggests that the system is useful in avoiding mandatory sentences imposed by statute for certain crimes (e.g., sale of narcotics) and thus is a way of tailoring sentencing to the needs of individual defendants. It has also been suggested that the plea-bargaining system limits the occurrence of trials to cases in which there are real issues of guilt. Thus, trials are reserved for "real" cases rather than being *pro forma* affairs in which the outcome is a foregone conclusion.

Another oft-cited argument—and one of particular interest here

—suggests that the defendant who admits his guilt deserves a more lenient sentence. This view suggests that admission of guilt is the first step toward rehabilitation, that acknowledgement of error is essential to eventual avoidance of antisocial conduct. Thus, the man who cops out is, in this view, deserving of lesser punishment because he has taken the first step toward acknowledging the legitimacy of the law, changing himself, and becoming "rehabilitated."

Another argument dealing with defendants' attitudes has recently been advanced in defense of plea-bargaining. This argument suggests that the system provides the defendant with a sense of efficacy: he actively participates in the decision about his punishment, and hence his dignity and sense of self-worth (and perhaps his respect for the law and the institutions of criminal justice) are increased.

> Whether the factors entering into the bargain are or are not meaningful as sentencing goals, they are at least visible to the defendant and his attorney. The defendant is able to influence the sentence, he may set forth bargaining factors and determine their relevance to the decision, and he may use his bargaining power to eliminate the grossest aspects of sentencing harshness and perhaps arbitrariness, be they legislative or judicial. The defendant, if he does not like the bargain, may reject it and stand trial. If he accepts the bargain, *he cannot help but feel that the sentence is something that he participated in bringing about, even if he at the same time resents the process that induced his consent.* And while he may find his "correctional treatment" brutal and meaningless on one level, his sentence is meaningful on another level in that at least he participated in it and influenced the final result. . . .
>
> The bargain may be looked at then, as an attempt by the defendant, and even by his counsel, to preserve their dignity in the process by finding a role for themselves even if it means a sentence based upon criteria logically irrelevant to the goals of the process.[7]

Before confronting the substance of the arguments dealing with defendants' attitudes, let us review briefly some of the general criticisms of bargain justice that have been offered. First, it is often argued that plea-bargaining subverts the basic notion of an adversary system. Instead of pitting the state against the individual in a contest in which the state must sustain its burden of proof and overcome the presumption of innocence, the plea-bargaining system sets aside questions of legal guilt and concentrates rather upon penalty. This not only has a tendency to demean the citizen, but also makes meaningless many of the procedural protections that are supposed to be afforded to defendants. Rules about interrogation, admission of evidence, hearsay testimony, and the like are submerged in a system in which defendants are encouraged not to exercise their rights. This argument assumes the distinction between factual and legal guilt: the difference between the questions "Did he do it?" and "Can the state *prove* that he did it, given a variety of constraints upon what is admissible evidence?" There is a great deal of confusion in our society about which concept ought to be of paramount importance. If factual guilt is the major issue, then plea-bargaining does not suffer in comparison with the full-blown adversary model, for the vast majority of defendants who plead guilty in return for some agreement are probably factually guilty. If, on the other hand, legal guilt is crucial—if the procedural protections are valued not simply for their truth-seeking ability but also because they place constraints upon the ability of law-enforcement officials to intervene in the lives of citizens—then plea-bargaining probably does weaken the force of these protections.

It has also been argued that the plea-bargaining system generally undermines the notion of rule by law:

> Plea negotiation has a marked advantage over traditional forms of adjudication in that it is a more flexible method of administering justice. It affords a far greater range of alternatives than do most trial proceedings. Flexibility is, however, an advantage that all lawless systems exhibit in comparison with systems of administering justice by rules. The utility of discretion must be balanced against the utility of pre-ordained rules, which can limit the importance of subjective judgments, promote equality, control corruption, and provide a basis for planning, both before and after controversies arise.[8]

A summary of other arguments against plea-bargaining is suggested by Enker:

> It bears a risk, the extent of which is unknown, that innocent defendants may plead guilty; negotiation becomes directed to

the issue of "how many years is a plea worth" rather than to any meaningful sentencing goals; factual information relating to the individual characteristics and needs of the particular defendant are often never developed; and a sense of purposelessness and lack of control pervades the entire process . . . it often gives the defendant an image of corruption in the system, or at least an image of a system lacking meaningful purpose and subject to manipulation by those who are wise to the right tricks. Cynicism, rather than respect, is the likely result.[9]

These criticisms all seem to me to have merit, although the focus of this book—the defendants' perspective—make some more salient than others. The criticisms that seem most basic in light of the defendants' perceptions deal with what Alschuler calls the "lawlessness" of the system. The system is, in the eyes of the defendants, lawless and lacking in the correct moral imperatives. The defendants find in the law itself a moral imperative that they are willing to embrace as valuable—although in their own behavior, in the ways in which they conduct their lives, they frequently find themselves violating these norms. When they do violate the law and happen to be caught, they do not find morality or principle guiding the behavior of those who are supposed to be enforcing the law. It is in this sense that the legal system is, in their eyes, lawless and immoral. For it closely resembles the world they live in on the streets, the world that many of them hate.

For this same reason the argument suggested by Enker above— that the defendant gains a sense of participation and acceptance by virtue of his participation in the plea-bargaining process—is mistaken. First, many of the men I spoke with had no real sense of participation. They waited in jail until their attorney brought an offer and felt compelled to take it for fear of getting something worse later. Moreover, implicit in the participation argument is the cooperation of attorney and client, working together to get the best deal. As we detail in the next chapter, most defendants represented by public defenders felt that their attorney was at best a middleman and more likely an agent of the state. It is much harder to "find a role" and be a participant when you see yourself as completely alone, when the putative member of your own team is in fact an opponent. Thus, for many of the men, the notion of being a participant determining one's own fate had little meaning. Operatively, many did not participate actively. Even when they did, I found little or no evidence that this participation—active bargaining—made their sentence more palatable. It is one thing to bargain actively and think that you got a "good deal"; it is another thing to assert that (as Enker hypothesizes) the sentence is therefore "meaningful."

Finally, and most importantly, Enker's hypothesis suffers from a basic misunderstanding of what the typical defendant wants from his encounter with the legal system. Defendants want something other than a sense of participation. I suggested in the chapter on police that many of the defendants recognize that what they do is not the behavior in which they *ought* to be engaging. They find themselves doing things that they *wish* they did not do. Many want someone— whether it be the police or the courts or doctors—to change them, to make them able to live without stealing or taking dope or injuring others. This is not simply "parole board talk." They want to participate in economic and social life in our society. Most aspire to the material symbols of worth that they see the middle class and rich possessing. They find themselves—and many others with whom they come into contact in their lives on the street—engaging in behavior that not only doesn't produce the material wealth they would like, but also involves breaking the law frequently, often getting arrested, and sometimes being sent to prison. What most desire is to be *different*. Participating in what sentence they get, affecting how much time they get in prison, does not help them attain this goal. The defendants don't know how to achieve it, nor, probably, do judges, prosecutors, or correctional administrators. But this is what the defendants want, and presumably so do members of the society at large.

Thus, most defendants would probably prefer *not* to participate. They would really prefer some ill-defined "they" to fix up their lives, to enable them to change and become different kinds of people. I do not mean to imply that most desire "brainwashing" or some fundamental changes in their personality or characteristics, though a few appear to desire such things. Rather, they wish that the general quality of their lives—especially their opportunities to participate effectively in economic life—could be changed so that they would not feel the need or incentive to engage in criminal conduct in order to satisfy their wants. To permit them to participate is, in a very real sense, to admit to the defendant that nobody really cares about him or knows what to do, to confirm that he has little hope. To let him participate—as the plea-bagaining system does—is to admit to him terrible failure.

Enker argues at another point, discussing sentencing of defendants who have not made a deal, that

> . . . in that moment of dread before a non-negotiated sentence is imposed, counsel at least, and probably the defendant have the feeling that they await the pronouncement of an arbitrary fiat which they are helpless to shape. The pronouncement of sentence, particularly if it is an unpleasant one, rarely mitigates this sense, for rarely does a judge articulate any reasons for imposing the sentence he has chosen other than to engage in an occasionally harsh speech excoriating the defendant and his like.[10]

This is no doubt true, for defendants don't like harsh sentences. In addition they would probably prefer a reasoned argument explaining the basis of their sentence to a "harsh speech." But I think his hypothesis is wrong in suggesting that defendants do not *want* an authoritative, externally imposed judgment; they might not object if only they had some confidence that the source of the "fiat" was actually acting in the defendant's interest. Because most judges, prosecutors, and correctional officials do not have the solutions to the defendant's problems, perhaps there is something to be said for getting the minimum sentence possible. But this argument constitutes a *rationalization* for the status quo, not really a *justification* for maintaining it. And if my impression of the defendants is correct they would prefer to have their fate decided by others who really had some "answers" to the difficulties that the defendant faces. They want some authoritative figure to care about them, to consider *why* they engage in criminal acts, and to prescribe some regimen that will enable them in the future to engage in law-abiding behavior.

---

1. See Richard Cass and Stuart Beck, "The Public Defender in Connecticut Circuit Court," unpublished manuscript, Yale Law School, 1971.

2. For a useful discussion of pretrial detention also dealing with Connecticut, see William A. Brockett, Jr., "Presumed Guilty: The Pre-Trial Detainee," *Yale Review of Law and Social Action,* I (1971), 10–27.

3. 400 U.S. 25 (1970).

4. See Harold Garfinkel, "Conditions of Successful Degradation Ceremonies," *American Journal of Sociology,* LXI (1956), 420–24.

5. Abraham Blumberg, *Criminal Justice* (Chicago: Quadrangle Books, 1967), p. 89.

6. The quotation is reprinted in Arnold Enker, *Perspectives on Plea-Bargaining,* President's Commission on Law Enforcement and Administration of Justice, Task Force Report: The Courts (Washington, D.C.: Government Printing Office, 1967), p. 112.

7. Ibid., p. 116. (Emphasis added.)

8. Albert W. Alschuler, "The Prosecutor's Role in Plea Bargaining," *University of Chicago Law Review,* XXXVI (1968), 71.

9. Enker, *Perspectives on Plea-Bargaining,* p. 117.

10. Ibid., p. 116.

4

The Defendant and His Attorney

In all criminal prosecutions, the accused shall enjoy the right
. . . to have the Assistance of Counsel for his defence.
Sixth Amendment to the Constitution

The right to be heard would be, in many cases, of little avail if
it did not comprehend the right to be heard by counsel. Even the
intelligent and educated layman has small and sometimes no
skill in the science of law. If charged with crime, he is incapable,
generally, of determining for himself whether the indictment is
good or bad. He is unfamiliar with the rules of evidence. Left
without the aid of counsel he may be put on trial without a proper
charge, and convicted upon incompetent evidence, or evidence
irrelevant to the issue or otherwise inadmissible. He lacks both
the skill and knowledge adequately to prepare his defense, even
though he have a perfect one. He requires the guiding hand of
counsel at every step in the proceedings against him. Without
it, though he be not guilty, he faces the danger of conviction because he does not know how to establish his innocence.
Powell v. Alabama, 1932

Governments, both state and federal, quite properly spend vast
sums of money to establish machinery to try defendants accused

of crime. Lawyers to prosecute are everywhere deemed essential to protect the public's interest in an orderly society. Similarly, there are few defendants charged with crime, few indeed, who fail to hire the best lawyers they can get to prepare and present their defenses. That government hires lawyers to prosecute and defendants who have the money hire lawyers to defend are the strongest indications of the widespread belief that lawyers in criminal courts are necessities, not luxuries. The right of one charged with crime to counsel may not be deemed fundamental and essential to fair trials in some countries, but it is in ours. From the very beginning, our state and national constitutions and laws have laid great emphasis on procedural and substantive safeguards designed to assure fair trials before impartial tribunals in which every defendant stands equal before the law. This noble ideal cannot be realized if the poor man charged with crime has to face his accusers without a lawyer to assist him.

Gideon v. *Wainwright*, 1963

Did you have a lawyer when you went to court the next day?

No. I had a public defender.   A *Defendant*, 1971

The words of the Constitution and the Supreme Court bespeak concern for a noble ideal, the fair trial. Integral to a fair trial is the provision of counsel for the defendant. A defendant's lawyer provides him with the advice necessary to a dignified and decent encounter with the legal system. Instead of standing alone, a defendant has at his side an attorney knowledgeable about the law and concerned with his welfare. Given the stressful and highly technical nature of the situation in which the defendant usually finds himself, a just system should permit him to have the advice and counsel of an attorney. If a society embraces the notion of equality between rich and poor, the indigent defendant should, as the rich man does, also enjoy this assistance.

During recent years the Supreme Court has evinced increasing concern for the rights of the accused. The touchstone of protection of these rights is representation by counsel. Without this resource even the most sophisticated defendant will not, so the argument goes, be in a position to exercise those rights that the Constitution provides.

Thus, the Court has held that defendants charged with serious crimes must be provided with defense counsel in both state and federal proceedings if they cannot afford to hire their own.[1] The importance of advice by counsel has led the Court to hold that indigents also enjoy the right to appointed counsel at various other stages of the criminal process, including interrogation by police officers, at a preliminary hearing, on appeal, and at a line-up.[2]

Two different systems for providing counsel to indigent defendants have been developed in this country: assigned counsel and public defenders. Assigned-counsel systems utilize attorneys appointed from the bar at large to represent indigent defendants. Thus, members of the bar volunteer (or, in some cases, are required) to be placed upon a list from which judges select attorneys to defend indigents. The attorney is usually paid a relatively small fee for his efforts. Two shortcomings of the assigned-counsel system have led many localities to adopt an alternative method, the public defender system. First, in some localities a few attorneys come to dominate the assigned-counsel systems. Because the fees for assigned-counsel work are small, these attorneys depend upon turning over large numbers of cases in order to earn their livelihood. Hence, they cannot or choose not to spend much time with any one defendant. When this problem does not arise, another often does. If the assigned counsel are drawn from a broad spectrum of the bar, many of the attorneys appointed to defend indigents may not be highly experienced in criminal law. Thus, junior associates from large corporate firms or lawyers specializing in real estate or probate may be called upon to defend criminal cases. Such attorneys usually do not have particular expertise in criminal law and may view their assigned-counsel work as uninteresting and distracting from their normal practices.

Partly in response to these two difficulties, many localities have established public or quasi-public agencies—often called public defender offices—to handle the defense of indigents. These attorneys are paid salaries by the state to defend poor clients. Thus, they specialize and presumably become expert in criminal law. Moreover, because they are paid salaries rather than fees for cases, they may not feel the economic pressure to turn over large numbers of cases that the private practitioner specializing in assigned-counsel cases encounters. Thus, the public defender is presumably both more expert and less subject to financial pressures than attorneys under assigned-counsel systems.

Connecticut has a public defender system, both for circuit and superior court (although different defenders serve each court). In addition, in some cities neighborhood legal assistance offices—funded by grants from the Office of Economic Opportunity, foundations, and a state agency—also provide counsel to indigent defendants. Thus, the defendants interviewed had one of three types of attorney: a public defender, a legal assistance attorney, or a private retained counsel. In this chapter we shall discuss relations between clients and all three types of lawyers.

The bulk of the men interviewed had been represented by a public defender (forty-nine of seventy-one). Several characteristics of the public defender system should be noted as a preface to our discussion of defendants' attitudes toward public defenders.

The public defenders in Connecticut superior courts—the subject of this discussion—have large caseloads. At any given time a public defender may be representing dozens of clients. Given his limited time and investigative resources, he cannot and does not spend very much time on any particular case. Equally important is the fact that the court system is itself a *social system*. The public defender "lives" with prosecutors and judges. He deals with them week in and week out, talking with them about cases, bargaining, perhaps socializing. His relationship to any one client is transient; his relationship to prosecutors, judges, and other court personnel is "permanent." Whether he gets on well with them or has an acrimonious relationship can significantly determine whether his job is enjoyable or full of conflict and frustration. This factor is crucial to understanding the behavior of the public defender and the defendants' perception of his role. The doctrine developed by the Supreme Court has concentrated upon providing an attorney for indigent defendants. Mechanisms to do so have been set up. But the behavior of the attorney and his relationship to his client are determined not simply by the theory of what the relationship between lawyer and client ought to be; the circumstances of the job that public defenders are called upon to perform are equally important.

In discussing the activities of attorneys who specialize in criminal work in the lower courts, Abraham Blumberg has observed:

The rules of due process, as expanded and strengthened by the Supreme Court, are predicated on the existence of an adversary system of criminal justice. The rules envision a "combative" procedural system wherein prosecution and defense (who are admittedly possessed of unequal resources) will clash. After the dust has settled, the data which determine innocence or guilt will have emerged. Unfortunately, this model of criminal justice does not exist in fact. At each stage of the process a tacit but erroneous assumption is made. It is assumed that the accused will ultimately have "his day in court." Oversights, mistakes of judgment, and the capricious behavior of enforcement officials will be carefully reviewed—by the next higher authority. This sort of individualization necessitated by due process introduces special complications in the daily work of the enforcement agencies, interfering with organizational values of efficiency and maximum production. . . . Note that counsel, whether privately retained or of the legal aid variety, have close and continuing relations with the prosecuting office and the court itself. Indeed, lines of communication, influence, and contact with those offices . . . are essential to the practice of criminal law. Accused persons come and go in the court system, but the structure and its personnel remain to carry on their respective career, occupational, and organizational enterprises. . . . Even the accused's lawyer has far greater professional, economic, intellectual, and other ties to the various elements in the court system than to his own client.[3]

One of the men interviewed suggested a similar view of the relationship between the public defender and the prosecutor:

If a court has a heavy caseload, it affects the prosecutor, the judge, and everybody concerned. Now, if they can ease this caseload by the prosecutor giving a few, the public defender giving a few, it's a little better for everyone concerned. Take, for instance, Mr. "Watkins" [the chief prosecutor in the district from which this man came]. Mr. Watkins runs his office, and Mr. "Stankowski," the head public defender, he runs his office, but no one can tell me that they're not on good terms or even friends. If not friends, they've got a nice working arrangement. They've been knowing each other for over ten years. They got to have respect for each other, so forth and so on. Now, I guess when they sit down and go over a bunch of cases, they say, Well, look at this guy, what are we going to do about him? You know he's guilty, but he's got this little technicality here; and it's true. I think the public defender sacrifice him, and in his opinion he justifies it by asking a favor to maybe a kid that he's guilty but he's not pleading guilty. He's going to cause a lot of stink, and because he's young, let's give him a break. They could go through the trouble of convicting him if they want. Always, I think, in a sense, one hand washes the other.

Thus, the behavior of the participants in the criminal process must be understood in the context of the relationships between its various members. Interpersonal relations, debts owed and receivable, the necessity to establish tolerable working relationships with those with whom one comes into daily contact are crucial aspects of the criminal justice process. None of these requires or necessarily implies that a public defender will sell out his client in the interest of harmony and amicable relations with judges and prosecutors. They do provide an explanation, though, for the role that the public defender appears to the defendants to play in keeping the system operating. When a defendant thinks of the public defender as one of "them" rather than as someone on "his" side he is, in an organizational sense, probably right. Most public defenders probably regret their inability to spend more time on individual cases and their role as a middleman or broker. The system to a large extent, though, imposes this role upon them. We will now examine in more detail the defendants' views of their attorneys. We will look at attorney-client relations among public defenders, legal assistance attorneys, and private retained counsel. As an overview let us look briefly at a simple set of numbers. All respondents were asked the following question: "Do you think [your lawyer] was on your side?" The responses of the defendants with different types of lawyers are as follows:

Type of Lawyer	Percentage Responding "Yes"
Public Defender	20.4 (10 of 49)
Private Retained	100.0 (12 of 12)
Legal Assistance	70.0 (7 of 10)

The simple statistics are rather startling. Nearly 80 percent of those represented by public defenders felt that their lawyer was not on their side. All those who had private attorneys felt that their lawyer was on their side. Legal assistance attorneys fared somewhere in the middle in their clients' evaluations. Although the numbers are too small to make statistical analysis useful, the responses to this question are not simply an artifact of how well a client did in his case. Although those who received suspended sentences or dismissals were somewhat more charitable toward their public defenders, the difference between the public defender and other attorneys remains. What is going on when four-fifths of the men defended by the public defender think that he does not represent them? Exploring the roots of defendants' attitudes toward their attorneys will further illuminate the consumer's perspective on criminal justice.

THE PUBLIC DEFENDER: MAN IN THE MIDDLE

Nearly 70 percent of the men interviewed were represented by the public defender. They had little choice in the matter: they did not have the money to hire a lawyer, and the judge appointed the public defender to represent them. A defendant typically encountered his lawyer in the hallway or bullpen (lock-up) of the courthouse, or else he found himself before the judge with a man beside him who turned out to be his attorney. The typical defendant reported that he spent a total of five to ten minutes conferring with his attorney, usually in rapid, hushed conversations in the courthouse. Thus, a man who may receive five or ten years in prison spends five or ten minutes with the man who is supposed to supply the "guiding hand of counsel," to ensure that his rights are exercised and protected, to make certain that the "noble ideal" of a fair trial is protected.

What can a defendant talk about in five to ten minutes with "his" attorney? His social and psychological background? His motives for committing the crime, if he did indeed do it? The nature of police investigation and interrogation and possible legal defenses dealing with search and seizure and entrapment? His goals and treatment needs? Hardly. What he can talk about is the deal. Most of the men reported that among the first words uttered by their public defender were: "I can get you————if you plead guilty." Perhaps they do not remember other words that came before, but certainly these were the most salient words the public defender uttered.

You know, his name in superior court is known as "cop-out Kujawski." This what everybody in prison calls him cause that's the first thing as soon as he comes in your cell in superior court, that's the first thing he says—cop out, cop out, cop out. Through the past years everybody's known him as cop-out Kujawski. He's earned a name for himself.

*   *   *

Well, he have the nickname of "cop-out Kujawski." That's all; it's the only thing that you hear from him: If you cop out, I get you this; if you cop out, I get you that. If you cop out, I get you a suspended sentence—that's the only thing he ever speak about. Other than that, he don't speak about—well, at first he might say, Well, I'm gonna try and do this for you—or do somethin like that; then maybe he might come back two or three weeks later, and he says, You cop out. That's what he always brings up—cop out—that's the first thing. If you cop out, I get you this—and that's it.

Thus, the public defender is not "their" lawyer, but an agent of the state. He is the surrogate of the prosecutor—a member of "their little syndicate"—rather than the defendant's representative.

He seemed like he didn't care one way or the other. He just cop out, you know. Like, you see a police walking on the street writing a ticket out, you know. He puts a ticket on the car. He don't care whose car it is. [The public defender] say, just, you know, You cop out to this, and you say no, and he says, I see if I can get a better deal. Then he brings another offer: You cop out to this. Just like that, you know. Just checking on the cop-outs.

*   *   *

A public defender is just like the prosecutor's assistant. Anything you tell this man, he's not gonna do anything but relay it back to the public defender [*sic*; he means the prosecutor];

they'll come to some sort of agreement, and that's the best you're gonna get. You know, whatever they come to and he brings you back the first time, well, you better accept it because you may get more.

* * *

He just playing a middle game. You know, you're the public defender; now, you don't care what happens to me, really. You don't know me, and I don't know you; this is your job, that's all; so you're gonna go up there and say a little bit, make it look like you're tryin to help me, but actually you don't give a damn.

* * *

It's just like you got a junkie there, and he needs a bag of dope, and you tell him, Well, here's the bag of dope if you want it, or you gotta suffer it out, if you want to, you know. I mean, here's the bag of dope if you want it; I mean, you don't have to take it, when you know damn well he gonna snatch at it, cause the man is sick, you know what I mean.

You say the public defender is like that?

Sure, [it's as if someone says to a junkie], Well, here's the bag of dope. If you want it, you can take it; if you don't. . . . Well, you say, Yeah, I want it, I want it, I'm sick, man. That's the way it is, man. It's nothing big to him. Like I say, he makes deals like this every day.

The public defender typically has access to police reports and knows the strength of the case against the defendant. Before any extended discussion with the defendant and the offer of a deal, he sometimes consults with the prosecutor and agrees on a tentative sentence in return for a plea. He knows what is "in the ballpark" for a particular offense given a man's record. He knows the man is guilty. He knows that failure to plead guilty will probably result in a conviction at trial and harsher punishment than can be obtained by a compromise and a guilty plea. He knows that his caseload is tremendous and that it is in the interest of the courts as a whole for most guilty men to plead guilty. He knows that he cannot spend as much time as he might like on any particular case.

Thus, the behavior of "their" attorney—especially if he is a public defender—contributes to the feeling that they are essentially standing alone without advice that they can rely upon to be impartial. This distrust of the public defender is terribly strong. Notice that in one of the excerpts reproduced above, a defendant said "public defender" when he meant to say "prosecutor." This mistake was common—at one point or another most of the men interviewed either called the public defender the prosecutor or called the prosecutor the public defender. This is a subtle but significant indicator of the confusion of roles that the defendants experienced—the near interchangeability of "their" lawyer with the prosecutor.

Unlike the private lawyer, who was viewed as giving advice, providing information and offering suggestions, most defendants felt that the public defender tried to tell them what to do. This is also a major source of dissatisfaction with the public defender. Another source of dissatisfaction stems from the lack of choice facing the typical defendant. The indigent defendant—except in those cities in which legal assistance lawyers handle criminal cases—is simply *given* the public defender. Most feel that they cannot *fire* their defender— he is simply given to them, and they have no control over the matter.

Although most defendants do not consider the possibility, they can in fact sometimes fire their public defender. Most either don't know that this is possible or think that they will simply get another of the same. Two of the men interviewed refused the services of the regular public defender and had special public defenders appointed from the private bar.* These two men were somewhat more satisfied with their attorneys, though both were in prison. Both reported that they felt their attorney was on their side, though both were quite bitter about their convictions and sentences. Both felt that they had a reasonably good relationship with their attorney and that they exchanged ideas rather than simply received instructions about how they ought to behave. Their attorneys apparently were able to spend somewhat more time with them than the public defender usually does. The fact that the defendants had some voice in the selection of their attorneys also seems to have been important. Both knew that but for their choice, the attorney would not have received the case and the

* A defendant may also receive a "special" public defender—a lawyer appointed from the bar at large—if he is one of a group of codefendants, another of whom is represented by the regular public defender.

money that went with it, though the money was admittedly rather meager. We shall return to this theme later, for the notion of choice —of some control over the lawyer's getting the case—seems an important determinant of a defendant's evaluation of his attorney's services.

Another factor contributing to distrust of the public defender is the belief that most public defenders desire to become prosecutors (and then, eventually, judges). As two men suggested: "The more convictions he get . . . and the higher he can get"; "Most of the prosecutors—most of the public defenders go from public defender to prosecutor." There are no systematic data available describing career patterns of public defenders, but it is by no means unheard of for a public defender to join the prosecutor's staff. Such incidents become widely known and are cited frequently as indicating that the public defender must be working with the prosecution in order to further his own career ambitions.

Another factor is that the public defender really has no financial incentive for fighting hard for his clients. "He gets his money either way," was the common phrase—whether his client wins or loses. The ability of a "street lawyer" (private attorney) to get clients depends upon his reputation, and defendants believe that good reputations are built by winning cases. The public defender, on the other hand, does not have to depend upon his reputation to get clients—he receives them automatically, whether he wins many cases or loses many. Thus, from a defendant's vantage point, the public defender has nothing to gain (and perhaps, given his perceived career ambitions, something to lose) by vigorously defending clients.

> Public defenders usually don't want to fight a case in this state. They get the same amount of money if they win or lose; so why should they fight if they don't have to, if they got an easy way out?

Perhaps the most important factor affecting defendants' distrust of the public defender is his position as an employee of the state: "They got to be on the state's side in order that they can work for the state." Most of the men with whom I spoke approach life with a simple yet powerful premise. Put in abstract form, it might be stated as follows: any two or more persons receiving money from a common source must have common interests. In the context of defendant-public defender relations, it urges that since both the prosecutor and the public defender are employed by "the state," they *cannot* fight one another. He who pays the piper calls the tune in this world, and if the same source is paying the public defender and the prosecutor, the reasonable expectation is that they will work together. Thus, a crucial difference between a street lawyer and a public defender is that the street lawyer is *paid* by the client; the public defender is not:

> You're giving him [a street lawyer] something for you. I wasn't giving "Jones" [a legal assistance lawyer] nothing, and what they're paying him, they're gonna pay him that anyway. [With a private lawyer] if he doesn't go for you, you give him half salary; you don't have to pay him his other half. And I think that he'll look at that a lot, you know.

* * *

> *Why is it that [street lawyers] do a better job for you?*
>
> Well, first of all, you payin him; so you got a right to demand some things.

* * *

> Because I feel that if you are paying a lawyer—regardless whether you wrong or right—the person he's defending come first. By hiring a lawyer, he'll take time cause I mean if you want to talk, he feel, Well, damn it, this man is paying me, he got a right to talk to me about it cause he want to know what's goin on, and you got to tell him. But on those terms you not payin him; so you really can't say nothin if you want to talk.

* * *

> You're paying [the street lawyer]; you're given him money, you're putting food—in other words, you know, you're gonna buy his next suit or maybe his next house. The public defender just can't possibly get—the one I got, he must not got too much pay from the state. I know he wasn't gettin no hundred dollars. Since, you know, he ain't making much money. If I only had a

thousand dollars hidden in my sock and I asked and I brung it out, he would have went and helped me more, you know.

Thus, paying a lawyer not only provides some assurance that he is on the defendant's side, but also gives the defendant a sense of leverage over his attorney, a sense that he is in a position of some autonomy. Most of the men had never had street lawyers and were simply expressing a faith that this is the way that it would be; the key to their analysis was the notion of a financial transaction between lawyer and client. By paying an attorney, you can make sure that he is "yours." We shall see in the next section that this feeling did in fact characterize those few defendants who were able to retain attorneys.

The importance of money and of financial transactions reflects the general socialization into a market economy that the defendants, like all Americans, have experienced. In this sense the defendants were very "good" Americans, for they were very accepting of the ethic of the marketplace. For example, although most felt that the poor fare worse than the rich in the legal system, they also believe that this cannot be changed. When asked whether they felt that a "society in which there weren't any rich and weren't any poor, but everybody had about the same" would be better or worse, a majority felt that it would be worse (or was, given human nature, unattainable). They want the opportunity to get rich themselves, to enjoy the benefits of life that others enjoy, and tend to associate equality with moving everyone down to the lowest common denominator.

Likewise, almost all—even those convicted of property crimes—were accepting and supportive of laws against taking property from others. After all, they reasoned, when I get rich I don't want someone taking it away from me. With only a couple of exceptions, none of the men was a modern-day Robin Hood taking from the rich to aid the poor (except in an individualistic sense—aiding himself), or a "radical" who believed that the rich had no "right" to possess what the poor cannot have. Most *wanted* what the rich have, but almost none felt that this made it morally right to steal from the rich. Indeed, the men seemed to have strongly internalized the marketplace ethic of our society. They believe that you get what you pay for and that what costs more is probably better than (or at least as good as) what costs less.

It is not surprising, then, that defendants who didn't have the money to purchase an attorney's services think that the "merchandise" which they were provided by the state was inferior to that available on the open market. In many ways, the crucial difference between the public defender and street lawyers lies not only in how they behave toward their clients—how much time they give them, how concerned they appear to be, how the case comes out—but also in the nature of the transaction between lawyer and client. Money talks:

> *Suppose you'd said to your public defender, "Here's a hundred dollars if you can get me a suspended sentence." Do you think he'd have fought any harder for you?*

> I'm almost positive he would. If you were a public defender— now you're only gettin paid by the state—and a guy said, "Look, if you can beat this case, I'll give you an extra hundred dollars on the side." . . . I mean, it's a hundred dollars, and all you gotta do is put a little more effort into it—just like anybody else would do, cause it's the next hundred dollars, and that's what he's tryin to do: he's trying to make as much money as he can.

Some of the men I spoke with had been represented by public defenders and had received suspended sentences. They were, not unnaturally, somewhat more satisfied with the quality of representation they had been afforded, though all expressed a preference in future cases for a street lawyer rather than a public defender. Moreover, they tended to attribute the "good" outcome not to their lawyer but to their own efforts ("I talked up to the judge and told him I was in the methadone program") or to luck. They generally refused to believe that their own attorneys were responsible for the outcome, for they did not really trust the public defender. Thus, even when the public defender did well for a client, he did not seem able to convince him that he had adequately represented him.

The common view among all men represented by the public defender was, then, "If only I'd had a street lawyer, I'd have come out much better." Yet looking at the charges against the defendants, their reports of the evidence against them, their past records, and the like, this expectation often appeared to be somewhat unrealistic, for many seemed to have come out fairly well. Men who expressed this desire for a street lawyer were asked whether they had ever had one. Most had not and were simply expressing blind faith in street lawyers and distrust of the public defender:

> *If you got in trouble again, would you like to be represented by this man [a public defender]?*
>
> No! I'm gettin a lawyer this time. I'm payin for a lawyer.
>
> *Well, a lot of guys tell me that they think that street lawyers do a better job for them than a public defender. Why do you think that's true?*
>
> Because you pay . . . I mean, like this guy [a private attorney with whom the defendant had had contact] said if I paid the three hundred dollars, he said he might of got me off on probation. He might have.
>
> *How do you think he could have done that if the public defender couldn't have?*
>
> I don't know!

Others, though, did have experiences with street lawyers, but the stories they told were quite mixed. A few spoke of "sure" convictions beaten by wily and dedicated street lawyers. Many described cases in which they appeared to have fared only moderately well—the outcome was about what one could expect—but which had cost them substantial sums of money. Some related stories in which it appeared that they had been exploited—their sentences were harsh, and the fee seemed exorbitant. But in almost all situations, even the last, the defendants spoke with a kind of satisfaction about the quality of their representation. Not that the outcome was always desirable, but at least they had *paid* the lawyer—he depended upon them for his money—and hence he must have been on their side.

The importance of money and of the financial exchange also emerged in the defendants' notions of the ideal relationship between lawyer and client. Most seemed to desire a contingent fee arrangement. A defendant would retain an attorney for a small fee and would pay him a further fee based on the outcome of the case (e.g., a thousand dollars for an acquittal or dismissal; five hundred dollars for a suspended sentence; three hundred dollars for a one-to-three-year sentence; one hundred dollars for a two-to-five). Such an arrangement may not make much economic sense, for the outcome may not vary directly with the amount of time spent on a case, but it indicates that defendants tend to associate the size of the exchange with the efforts of the attorney.

The relationship of public defender to client seems to the defendants another perversion of the symbols of the criminal justice system. The gamelike nature of the proceeding extends even to the defendant's *own* lawyer, for he is himself playing a game, mediating between prosecutor and defendant, pursuing interpersonal and professional goals that are seen as contrary to the goals of the defendant, whom the lawyer is supposed to be representing.

STREET LAWYERS: WHAT YOU PAY FOR IS YOURS

A few of the men interviewed were represented by private attorneys. Defendants who had had the service of private attorneys were unanimous in believing that their attorney was on their side, even though nine of the twelve ended up in prison. By definition those with private attorneys were differentiated from others by greater access to money. Most were sons of lower-middle- and middle-class parents who helped them pay for their attorney.

An entirely different aura surrounded the defendant's notions of his relationship with his attorney. In part, this sense of greater satisfaction was the product of different behavior by their attorney. Enjoying substantially lighter caseloads, the private attorney was reported to have spent much more time with his client.* Unlike the public defenders, the private attorneys were reported to have visited

---

* In some states low-level "courthouse" criminal lawyers hang around courthouses offering their services to poor defendants for relatively low fees. These attorneys are generally highly exploitative—turning over cases quickly to generate their fees. See Blumberg, *Criminal Justice*. Because of the public defender system and the availability of some criminal attorneys from legal services programs, this type of lawyer does not seem prevalent in Connecticut.

clients in jail and to have spent time discussing the case with the client.

As noted in the preceding section, most men represented by the public defender felt that he attempted to tell them what to do, rather than discuss the case and simply make suggestions. Most of those represented by private attorneys felt that their attorney had not tried to "muscle" them, but had merely made suggestions about what they ought to do; moreover, when a lawyer was insistent about a point, the defendant was much more inclined to accept it as an exercise of proper authority rather than as the imposition of will. This acceptance seems to be the product both of the general sense of efficacy that paying a lawyer seems to bring and of the fact that they trusted the advice that the lawyer gave them.

> He made it a point always to see me either before or after court and explain. . . . If it was before court, he'd explain what was going to take place and what he was going to say and how he would present himself; and if he didn't get a chance to see me before court, after court he'd always come down and see and say, Well, did you understand this, did you understand that; and if I said no, he'd explain it to me, you know, what went on.

> *Thinking back over your dealings with your lawyer, do you feel that he generally took instructions from you or told you what to do?*

> Think a little bit of both. He never dictated to me what to do, but I think he kind of used his knowledge and experience to kind of guide me along. And tell me where he thought I'd be making a mistake or help me plan a course of action.

> *Can you give me an example of that, of where he guided you along where you might be mistaken?*

> Where he advised me to plead guilty. He told me the reasons why he felt I should, but again he told me to do what I thought was right. I really think he was trying to help me. Because he told me that he didn't believe I could beat the case. So he said that he would try to mitigate the sentence as much as possible. He said he'd do anything in his power to help me out. And the impression that he gave me was that he was doing just that. And you know, if I ever have any further dealings with the law—not

necessarily criminal, I mean, if I ever want to file some sort of suit or anything—I think I'm going to look for him in the future.

*   *   *

He more or less told me what to do because for one thing I don't know too much about the law, to instruct a lawyer really —but no, I rather take that back. He didn't exactly tell me what to do. He laid things on the line. He told me this can happen, and this can happen; so what we got to do is make up our minds. What I would do if I don't understand what can happen, like you can say, "Well, you can get a five-to-six because you sellin narcotics." And I say, "Well, why do I have to take a five-to-six, because I know other cases where they been gettin lesser time?" He explained to me how the laws working, and what they doing up there in superior court. So he didn't more or less tell me what to do. He explained what can happen and what couldn't happen, and I would make my judgment.

*   *   *

He suggested things, and I made the final decision. He did the talkin, and I told him what to do—what I wanted.

This is not to say that all defendants with street lawyers were completely satisfied with their attorneys. None wanted to be in prison, and most of them were. Some didn't care for their lawyers personally, finding them cold or brash. Some felt that the attorney had other things on his mind and hadn't paid as much attention to their cases as he might have. Some felt that their attorneys were not as skilled in the criminal law as they might have been, and others felt unable to communicate as well as they wished. But still, they took it as a kind of *given* that the lawyer was on their side. This feeling is obviously in part the product of the behavior of the attorney, for the street lawyers seem to have spent more time and appeared more concerned with their clients.

But I think that the nature of the relationship of lawyer to client depends upon more than simply how the lawyer behaves. The nature of the transaction between attorney and client provides a context for *interpreting* the behavior of the attorney. In part because the defendant (or his family) was *paying* the attorney, the whole tone of the relationship was altered. For example, insistence upon a particular course of action by a street lawyer (e.g., pleading guilty, commitment for observation to a hospital) is interpreted differently by his client. Similar "advice" from a public defender might well be interpreted as giving orders, as telling the client what to do rather than discussing it with him. With a street lawyer the insistent advice is only the lawyer's "proper" role and the exercise of the expertise that he is supposed to possess.

The greater sense of efficacy exhibited by defendants with street lawyers may in part be a product of their general lifestyles. Since they had some money or came from families with money, they were more used to the notion of employing someone to do work for them. In their everyday lives, unlike those who were poorer, they were not as used to being treated as objects by more powerful "others," such as police officers, social workers, welfare officials, and the like. Hence, they brought to their encounter with an attorney a sense of dignity and efficacy that affected their relationship.

But, again, I think that the exchange is quite important. Recall the two men who had "special" public defenders appointed for them. Both exhibited a sense of efficacy quite like that exhibited by defendants with private attorneys. This seems to have been the product of *choice*, of having participated in deciding who would be their attorney. The man with a private attorney not only has choice, but also *pays*. He is giving the lawyer something, and this puts him on a footing firmer than that of supplicant.

LEGAL ASSISTANCE ATTORNEYS: WHY DO THEY DO IT?

A few of the defendants interviewed had been represented by attorneys from New Haven Legal Assistance. This organization—supported by the Office of Economic Opportunity, state funds, and foundation grants—operates out of neighborhood legal offices and offers a variety of legal services to poor people. In addition to handling a variety of civil matters, legal assistance attorneys also represent clients in criminal proceedings. Like the public defender, the legal assistance attorney (LAA) receives a salary for his legal work rather than fees for individual cases. In fact, until recently the bulk of LAA funds for criminal representation came from the state; so the LAA lawyer was paid by the same source as the public defender, though the connection was much more tenuous and less salient.

In other respects the LAA attorneys are quite different from the public defender. The attorneys enjoy much less cordial relationships with judges and prosecutors than the public defender does. They are generally viewed as being less willing to bargain and to be cooperative, and have something of a "troublemaker" image among other court personnel.[4] They are much more likely to file motions in behalf of their clients—motions to dismiss charges, to have probable-cause hearings, to suppress evidence. Such motion work is perceived by judges to be often frivolous, though there is some very tentative evidence that LAA attorneys might be more successful than the public defender in having charges dismissed.[5] Thus, the posture of the LAA attorneys toward the courts and the prosecution is, in general, somewhat more confrontation oriented, though many of their clients do plead guilty.

The LAA attorneys differ in two other important respects. First, they were *chosen* by the defendant. Most defendants who had LAA attorneys could have been represented by the public defender, but chose LAA instead. Second, LAA attorneys doing criminal work have somewhat lighter caseloads than the public defenders. They are able to spend more time with their clients and sometimes make visits to jail, something public defenders rarely do.

Thus, the LAA attorneys are somewhere between the public defender and the private attorney. They are not paid, but are chosen; they have more time to spend with clients; they are, in a sense, employees of the state, but in a very tenuous fashion. The reactions of defendants to LAA attorneys illuminate the factors that go into evaluations of the adequacy of counsel.

Defendants represented by LAA attorneys were somewhat equivocal—and, to an extent, confused—about the services rendered by their lawyer. All the defendants had consciously chosen to be represented by LAA, many because they had been represented by them in the past in either civil or criminal matters, and felt that they would do a better job than the public defender:

He did me better than them public defenders, you know. If I would of had a public defender, man, the prosecutor [would have] talked him right down. I was messin around in the jail with one of them guys [i.e., had been in contact with a public defender during a visit to the courthouse] . . . [but] they're all for the state. They're working for the state; they're just with the state, you know.

The defendants represented by legal assistance lawyers generally felt that their attorneys were more interested in them, fought harder for them, were more often on their side. At the same time, though, many were somewhat confused about the reasons for this concern and suspicious of it. This is not to say that they felt that the legal assistance lawyers were feigning concern, but simply that—in the absence of payment to the attorney—they found his concern rather puzzling. A few attributed this concern to ideological commitment on the part of the lawyers:

> Do you think the legal assistance guys are more on the side of their clients than the public defenders are?
>
> Right. Right. I know that. You know, they put more interest in; they put a lot of interest in.
>
> How do you account for that? Why do you think they're more interested in their client?
>
> I guess they feel in a way that—in fact, I know I might just be right—they feel the way that the people who can't pay for private—good lawyers—that they can help them out the best they can, just as good as a good lawyer.

Others attributed the greater activity and concern to the lighter caseloads that they think the legal assistance lawyers enjoy.

Although most perceived their attorneys to be interested and fighting hard for them, this reaction was tempered by some ambivalence. First, three of ten felt that the legal assistance lawyer was not on their side. Second, the majority of defendants—again in contrast to those with private attorneys—felt that their attorney attempted to tell them what to do rather than take instructions from them or engage in discussion and mutual decision. Given their descriptions of their interactions with their attorney, this view seems some-what anomalous, and I think it is in large measure a product of the fact that they were not paying their attorneys. A final indication of their ambivalence toward the legal assistance lawyers was the fact that all but one of the men interviewed indicated that, should they get in trouble again, they would prefer a private attorney to a legal as-sistance lawyer (though all preferred legal assistance to the public defender):

If you got in trouble again, would you like to be represented by [the same attorney]?

Me? Heck, no. If I'd of . . . if I'd of paid for a lawyer, I know I could have gotten a better sentence, you know, lesser time.

Why do you think a street lawyer would have done a better job?

Because you're giving him something for you. I wasn't giving [him] nothing.

*   *   *

If you got in trouble again, would you like to be represented by her?

I'd prefer to be represented by [another legal assistance attorney], you know, but I'd take her, unless of course I had money, in which case I'd go to a private lawyer.

Do you think private lawyers are better than public defender or legal assistance lawyers?

Yeah, I think so because I think they have more connections.

*   *   *

Would you like to get [this legal assistance lawyer] again?

No. I think I'd rather have my own lawyer, if I could have. I'd have more security then, you know, like—between that, I'd think about it, how he'd represent me.

So you wouldn't like him just because he's too busy?

Well, if he was [not] a free lawyer—if he wasn't a public de-fender or a legal aid—I would take him again.

In understanding the defendants' reactions to legal assistance lawyers, it is important yet difficult to sort out the various factors that produce their evaluations: the legal assistance attorneys did seem to the defendants to be more interested in them, to fight harder for them though, like the public defender, the lawyers were quite busy; the client felt that he had, to some extent, a say in choosing his attorney, for he could have been represented by the public defender instead; the defendant did not pay the attorney.

I think this last fact is of great importance in understanding the defendants' views of the legal assistance lawyer and their preference for street lawyers even when they were apparently quite satisfied with the way in which their legal assistance lawyer handled them and their case. The last man quoted above would like to have the same attorney, *if* he was a paid lawyer. This is not simply the product of a belief that paid lawyers are less busy. It is a product of the feeling that this is the way in which one can be *sure* of the lawyer's intentions. Moreover, as noted above, the feeling among many of the legal assistance clients that their lawyers told them what to do seems somewhat anomalous. When they were describing their relationships with their lawyer, they described interchanges much more like that between a defendant and a private attorney than between a client and a public defender. The lawyer seemed to have laid various alternatives before the client and indicated what he felt the best course was, but to have engaged in much less overt pressuring than was reported by defendants represented by public defenders. Yet the legal assistance clients tended to interpret this behavior as giving orders.

This interpretation stems, I believe, from the nature of the transaction between lawyer and client: their position as a kind of supplicant leads them to interpret their attorney's advice as orders. From talking with legal assistance lawyers, it seems clear that they consciously attempt to give a client a feeling that he is an individual deserving of dignity and respect. Yet the combination of the fact that the lawyers are quite busy and that the client does not pay them tends to make the defendant both somewhat suspicious of the lawyer's concern and doubtful whether he is his lawyer's partner or equal. The lawyer's more obvious interest makes the legal assistance attorney much more attractive than the public defender, but he is by no means the equal of the street lawyer. The marketplace ethic leads defendants to believe that what is free simply *cannot* be so good as what you must pay for. This very powerful consideration seems at the root of the suspicion of both the public defender and the legal assistance attorney. It is in part meliorated by the posture and behavior of the legal assistance lawyer, but not by any means eliminated.

ATTORNEYS, CLIENTS, AND CRIMINAL JUSTICE

We have examined the relationships between clients and three kinds of lawyers, attempting to detail the perceived posture of the lawyer and the determinants of defendants' evaluations of their legal representation. We began with the ideal of the attorney as servant of his client, offering him advice in a situation of extreme emotional stress and technical complexity, redressing the balance between the defendant and the state, and protecting both the interests and dignity of the men to whom the state attempts to apply the criminal sanction. The views of the defendants discussed here bear small resemblance to this ideal image, with the notable exception of those represented by private attorneys. For the bulk of the defendants—represented by public defenders—their attorney appeared to be at best a middleman and at worst an enemy agent.

This preliminary exploration of defendants' evaluations of their legal representation has focused upon the nature of the transaction between lawyer and client as a crucial determinant of the defendants' evaluations of their attorneys and of the fairness of the proceedings against them. We have argued that it is the lack of choice of attorney and of a financial exchange that contributes greatly to defendant distrust of the public defender and even of the more sympathetic and zealous legal assistance lawyers.

There is no system providing counsel to indigents that will convince the poor that they are receiving legal representation equal to that afforded to the rich. The argument advanced here, though, does suggest that if we are interested in providing defendants with a sense that they have not been alone, that they have been represented and treated by their attorney as someone who matters, then we must do more than simply provide a greater number of public defenders. Larger numbers of public defenders might be able to spend more time with clients, might be less infected with the production ethic that enormous caseloads produce. But they would remain direct employees of the state, and this fact alone may produce distrust by defendants. Perhaps experiments with systems (of which legal assistance is one model) in which the connection between the lawyer and the state is less obvious might be worth attempting. Another alternative, which would probably be extremely expensive, would involve the development of voucher systems. The defendant might be given something like a chit and then permitted to hire his own attorney. Such systems would move toward the literal transaction between lawyer and client that seems so important in convincing the defendant that he has a lawyer on his side. Such systems would perhaps provide defendants with the needed feeling that, but for *their* choice, the lawyer would not have gotten the case or the money. In order to prevent the possible domination of voucher systems by a few attorneys handling large numbers of voucher clients, perhaps a combination of the voucher and assigned-counsel systems might be attempted. A panel of lawyers from a broad spectrum of the bar willing to take criminal cases would be provided to a defendant along with his voucher. He could then select from the list and engage in a transaction with the lawyer he chooses.

The expense of such experiments may make them prohibitive, for the economies of scale introduced by public defender offices are enormous. But if we are truly concerned with a defendant's perspective, with his sense that his encounter with the criminal justice system has been equitable, something must be done to remove the feeling that the defendant stands alone. We have detailed in this and the previous chapter the activities of the system that lead the defendant to feel that he is an object being processed by people who don't have very sound notions of what they are up to, except to keep the assembly line operating. If the system of criminal justice is to teach defendants lessons about different modes of living, if it is to make them less likely to engage in "antisocial" conduct, it must not only treat them fairly but also give them the feeling that they have been treated fairly. We have attempted to point out here how the public defender system—in one jurisdiction—simply does not perform this function. If, as the Supreme Court so nobly stated in the *Gideon* opinion, "the right of one charged with crime to counsel" is deemed "fundamental and essential to fair trials" in our country, this right must have some real meaning—meaning not only from the viewpoint of legal standards about what constitutes adequate representation, but also in the eyes of defendants themselves. Currently our system does not appear to offer meaningful defense to indigents. It must if we are to convince defendants that they are being treated not as "files" to be closed but as human beings.

---

1. *Gideon* v. *Wainwright*, 372 U.S. 335 (1963).

2. *Escobedo* v. *Illinois*, 378 U.S. 478 (1964); *Miranda* v. *Arizona*, 384 U.S. 436 (1966); *White* v. *Maryland*, 373 U.S. 59 (1963); *Douglas* v. *California*, 372 U.S. 535 (1963); *United States* v. *Wade*, 388 U.S. 218 (1967).

3. Blumberg, *Criminal Justice*, pp. 26, 47.

4. Cass and Beck, "The Public Defender in Connecticut Circuit Court."

5. Ibid.; James Douglas, "A Comparison: Disposition of Criminal Cases Defended by Public Defenders and Legal Assistance Association Attorneys in New Haven, Connecticut," unpublished manuscript, Yale University, 1971.

5

Prosecutors and Judges

We turn now to the final participants in the criminal justice process of concern here: prosecutors and judges. These men represent "the state," the force that is attempting to punish the defendant, to take away his freedom, and put him in jail. Both of them possess enormous power over the defendant once he has been arrested and charged. How they exercise their power largely determines what will happen to him: whether he will be exonerated, found guilty, put on probation, or sent to prison. Each of these figures has not only power but also discretion. Within very loosely defined limits a prosecutor can, should he wish, simply refuse to proceed against a person charged with a crime. His decisions affect, as we have discussed before, what charges the defendant faces and thus the penalties that he may face. The prosecutor, moreover, typically makes a recommendation to the judge about proper punishment for a convicted man, and his recommendation is usually followed. Many defendants believe, in fact, that the prosecutor rather than the judge is the crucial figure in criminal justice, and they are probably correct.

The prosecutor and the judge are officers of the law, and responsibilities accompany their power and discretion. They play a crucial role in the determination of who is guilty and who is innocent. They must decide whether society's interest is served by proceeding against a particular defendant. They are responsible for protecting the legal rights of defendants, for making sure that evidence illegally obtained is not used against him. They must decide together what rehabilitative treatment will serve the interests of the defendant and society at large.

They have these interests in common, but also have somewhat different roles. The prosecutor is, literally, an attorney whose client is the state. He is hired and paid by the state to prosecute cases against those charged with crime. Although he is not supposed to prosecute men whom he feels are innocent, his role is very much that of advocate. He is not a neutral figure, even in theory, but the lawyer for the state. Good prosecutors are supposed to exercise their discretion in the interests of justice, but they are not supposed to be the ultimate arbiters of who is innocent or guilty and of who must go to prison and who may go free.

The judge is, in theory at least, the central figure of criminal justice. Sitting magisterially in his robes, literally above the other figures in the courtroom, he is, in popular images if not reality, the man who runs the show. Embodying the "law" and justice, he is supposed to be a truly neutral figure. Impartial between defendant and prosecution, he must referee their struggle, taking his cues from the law and from basic notions of decency and justice. He must see that the substance of the law is vindicated, that the guilty are convicted and punished and the innocent are set free. Moreover, he must see that the canons of due process are followed. Unlike the defendant's attorney or the prosecutor, the judge is partial only to the dictates of justice and the law. He is not indifferent, for he serves truth and justice and law—but he has no "client" in the way that an attorney does. His role at the preconviction phase is that of neutral arbiter. When sentencing a man, he is supposed to consider carefully the needs of the defendant and those of society and render judgment that maximizes the interests of each.

These are noble ideals. They may be straw men in the eyes of sophisticated observers of American criminal justice, but they are continually presented to citizens in school, in books, in movies, on television. Whether they are straw men or not, these noble ideals seem to have little relation to the reality of American criminal justice, and the defendants, perhaps more than anyone else, know it. The divergence from these ideals is the product of many things—of excessive caseloads, of a production ethic, of interpersonal relationships that develop in the court as a social system, of personal preferences and prejudices, of human failings. The stark contrasts between the theory of how these men *ought* to behave and the ways in which defendants see them behave emerge clearly and should be troublesome not only to the defendants themselves but also to anyone concerned with American justice.

PROSECUTORS

The defendants consistently believe that the prosecutor is the central figure in the operation of the criminal justice system. His is the power to determine their fate. Although many decisions by the prosecutor are formally within the power of the judge to alter, this is thought to occur infrequently. The prosecutor is the man to see; bargaining with him (and with the defendant's attorney) is the key to determining how well one emerges from his encounter with the legal system. What is the prosecutor up to? What is he after?

He might very well be seen as the enemy, as a villain whose intentions are to harm the defendant. This view of the prosecutor emerged occasionally ("he was out to get me") but was not the predominant mode of looking at the prosecutor. Rather, like the police officer, the prosecutor is seen as a worker, and he tries to do his job as efficiently as possible. The defendants are aware of the burdensome caseloads with which most prosecutors must deal. Thus, to get his job done, he must make deals. He cannot (or else does not much care to) spend much time on any given case. Rather, he must get it over with so that he can get on to the next:

> *Let me ask you a few questions about the prosecutor in your case. How do you think he saw his job? Think he was interested in giving you a fair shake, punishing you, getting rid of the case?*
>
> He wanted a conviction.
>
> *Why? Cause it makes him look good?*
>
> No, not really. No, it don't make him look good. Like nobody knows about it, you know. Who really cares if I'm guilty or not?

It's just like it might help him a little bit more in getting a better job; but, you know, with all the convictions he got, little convictions like mine don't really mean nothing. Cause any prosecutor can get that. But he might of thought that I was guilty, I don't know. I think the prosecutor goes along with most of what the police does or said. I don't think a prosecutor will, say, sit down and read the case over and he'll say, Police was wrong—because they only got one side of it. Like if I get arrested for anything—like anybody get arrested for anything—they can't prove themselves until they get into court. You know, like the police got, they shoot all their evidence to the prosecutor, like he got all the one side, what he did. I think he see most people come in front of him—maybe everybody that comes in front of him—is guilty. All he see is them being guilty because he got the evidence that show the guilt, if any. That they're arrested—he figures, It's my job to see that they stay in jail.

Why do you think he sees his job that way, rather than sort of looking at it independently and saying, he's innocent: we'll let him go. He's guilty: we ought to prosecute him?

I don't think that. I think that's all like this loose business, television shit where you see people, you know, fair play and what not. Everybody's thinking, when you're in that courtroom, everybody's thinking for theirselves, man. They thinking that's their job, man. Anything they see in there get them a better position, they get it, do it. So small cases, like I said before, don't help his position too much, but it helps some. But I don't think he'll be looking at where it's going to be fair or not; I think he's looking at it whereas he can get a conviction, you know.

Is it the kind of man who becomes a prosecutor or what the job does to him?

No, I don't think it's so much what the job does to him or what it takes to be a prosecutor. It's just like anything—like when you get a job, you start working on it. You start working on it, and it's a job, that's all. It's not nothing else, just your paycheck every week. When he go home, I don't think he be, you know, thinking about, saying, Man, I sent a man to prison for seven years; seven years, man, he got to be there for seven years. I don't think he be saying that if he gotta do life. I don't think he's going to cheer; he don't think on that. He see you—your face is just like this [other] man's face. Like every day, you walking down the street, you see somebody, you don't think of their face next week. He don't think about faces next week.

This account expresses well the view of the prosecutor as worker. His job is to get convictions, and to do so helps him because it is an indication that he is doing his job effectively. Advancement in his career (eventually leading to what defendants believe is the premier plum of the legal system, a judgeship) is his goal, and obtaining convictions is the way to do so:

What about the prosecutor? How do you think he saw his job? Do you think he was interested in giving you a fair shake? Punishing you? Getting rid of your case?

No, all a prosecutor is interested in is getting a conviction. That's his main thing. That's all they're interested in, getting a conviction. He just wanted to give me time. See, a lot of times it isn't that they don't like you; they don't even know you. But their job is to convict you, and that's it; that's what they want to do.

*   *   *

I don't think the prosecutor cares either, cause I think they've been doin it so long that it's become a part of 'em. I think they job is to convict a person, you know? They been doin it so long that it's just become a part of 'em.

*   *   *

That's their job—for a prosecutor, I guess—they're with the state, you know. The state's trying to convict you of something.

*   *   *

He has to do that, you know; he has to prove the defendant guilty. That's his job. Like, I didn't know—I had nothin against him.

Some defendants expressed a kind of resentment against the prosecutors for not listening to them personally, for not investigating their cases thoroughly enough. But the predominant view was not so much one of overt hostility as of a simple recognition that the prosecutor had a job to do and did it. The prosecutor not only wants convictions but also wants to get them as expeditiously as possible, for he has many cases to handle:

> They try to get rid of these cases as quick as possible because the jails are overcrowded, and a lot of guys are waiting to go to higher court in jail.

*   *   *

> He don't care who he hurts or who feets he step on. The biggest thing he wants to do is get to be in the judge's seat. He wants to be where he can be the king. He's [a] disciple down there now; so then he wants to go up there where he can be king. Once he get where he can be king, he can say, I can send you away for life—whatever I want to do, I can do it.

*   *   *

> Maybe he's trying to climb up the political ladder. Yeah. Or maybe he feels that having an outstanding record, you know, as far as sending people to the penitentiary, maybe he thinks that'll help him.

*   *   *

What about the prosecutor in your case? What do you think he was trying to do? Give you a fair shake? Punish you? Get rid of the case as quickly as possible?

Yeah, they have a young prosecutor, real young prosecutor, and like I told you, somebody had to go to jail. They had that young prosecutor in there, and he was gonna make sure somebody go to jail.

Why did somebody have to go to jail?

Well, we in superior court now. How many people do you know that leave superior court? For anything? Not too many. They goin to jail or get probation or something. Now, [the] three of us ain't gonna leave that court. They got a young prosecutor, and he got no choice *but* to—he tryin to build his life up, to make things look good for him. He got a family.

It makes him look good if people go to jail?

> It makes him look good if he bring up all kinds of points, make
> the court think that he know what he doin. He don't want to
> look like a fool—there's three young men up here, and he can't
> send *one* of them to jail. This man ain't nothin.

These goals and the worker's ethic mean that he will make deals
in order to get his convictions as expeditiously as possible. The deals
that he will accept are determined, the defendants believe, by a
variety of factors. Most important is a kind of "ballpark" figure (the
phrase was suggested to me by a public defender) for each offense.
The "ballpark's" dimensions are determined by the statutory penalties
and also, crucially, by a defendant's past criminal record. Thus, there
is a going rate for a given crime, which may be modified on the basis
of the extent of a man's previous record. In addition to this general
norming factor, deals are affected by what the market at any time will
bear. If the courts and jails are especially crowded, better deals are
probably in the offing. If things are slow, then the prosecutor will
drive harder bargains. In addition to the market in general, the defendant himself may be able to adjust the ballpark figure at the
margins. If he is tenacious, if he holds out, then the prosecutor's
desire to get things over with—as a worker, he does not like "un-
finished" products cluttering up the workshop—may cause him to
make an especially good deal.

Other factors may sometimes be crucial. One is public pressure.
If there is intense dislike of a crime, then the prosecutor may change
the "ballpark" in response to such pressure:

> This narcotic thing has got[ten] to be just a outrage thing.
> There's just so much of it that I feel the prosecutor really tries
> to put you away, get you off the street. They feel you're a
> menace to the street; so I feel the prosecutor really tries to get
> you convicted.

Another factor is connections: if your attorney is well connected, he
may be able to get you a better deal than one could normally expect
given the nature of the crime and a man's past record. The prosecutor

may owe your attorney a favor for a past case, and it may be repaid in your case.

Thus, the decisions of the prosecutor are determined by a variety of factors that produce a general norm of some certainty, though some deviations—on the good or bad side—are also common. As many of the defendants notice and resent, the factors that produce the outcome in their cases—what deal the prosecutor decides to make—seem in large part to have little to do with *them*. This fact rankles many, for it seems to cut against their desire to change and against the rhetoric of the system that they have been taught.

Oh, I think [the prosecutor] had an idea of the sentence I would get, you know. They know, but did he care? No, I don't think he *cared* especially. He knew I was guilty; I told him I was guilty. If he read my case, which he might of, then I don't think he gave a goddamn about rehabilitation; but I don't think it had anything to do with me. I don't really understand prosecutors. Is a prosecutor an appointed thing for a certain period of time? Yeah, that's what I thought. I think it's that he's got a job—he's got to do it. Sometimes you get somebody who's a dedicated lawyer, and they're gonna do what they think is right; sometimes you get somebody who's a shyster. But you get what you get, and this guy in particular? My case was no big thing; it's a pretty average run of the mill case. I pleaded guilty. I didn't think he's gonna get too involved about it.

*   *   *

I don't think [the prosecutor] had to offer that much time. Cause I never did no time before, you know. I don't think he should of gave me that much.

Why do you think he did?

I don't know. There was a lot of tension going at the time, too, when I got arrested. They had just pulled a drug raid and they pulled in thirty-eight, thirty-nine people, you know, and they're interested in cleaning up the streets. So, that might have been it; I don't know.

We have alluded before to the notion of fairness in the defendants' evaluations of their sentences. The men interviewed had some difficulty applying this concept to their experience. In part this is so because "fairness" in a matter like sentencing is a highly individualistic concept—a "fair" sentence presumably depends upon a large number of characteristics, including the nature of the offense, the harm done, the statutory penalties possible, the motives of the offender, his rehabilitative needs, the likelihood that he will engage in similar behavior in the future. Many of the defendants did not apply such a notion when asked about their sentences. Likewise, they tended to respond to questions about whether prosecutors were "fair" simply in terms of how well they came out, of the relationship between the maximum harm that could have been done to them and what penalty they actually had to pay.

Do you think this prosecutor in your case was fair to you?

To some extent, to some extent, yes, because I think I got a pretty good break.

*　　*　　*

Yeah, he was fair. I got a fair deal on it. I got eight months. I could of got bounded over and got more.

This is another indication that the system, as seen by the defendants, does not look at them as people, but rather as objects. Fair is simply doing well, regardless of what you are like. Again, the defendants are probably not wrong in their views of what is being done to them. In a discussion of prosecutors, Alschuler notes:

> Administrative considerations are far more basic. "We are running a machine," a Los Angeles trial assistant [prosecutor] declares. "We know we have to grind them out fast." An assistant state's attorney in Chicago notes that there are more than twenty-five hundred indictments currently pending in the Cook County Circuit Court, the greatest number in history. He says, "I'll do anything I can to avoid adding to the backlog." A Houston trial assistant observes, "We moved more than two thousand cases through six courts during the past three months; clearly the most important part of our job lies in making defendants think they are getting a good deal." [1]

Certainly the large majority of men I spoke with did not think they had received terrible "deals," though many wished they had been better. But they also know that the prosecutor is in fact attempting to make them "think" something in order to get rid of them and on to the next case. Some are resigned to this and simply accept it; others resent it deeply. In both cases, though, the effects of this knowledge upon their respect for the system, for their sense of self-worth and dignity, and for the lesson they learn from their experience with criminal justice are again not what we would wish to be teaching. What does making a defendant think he has gotten a good deal have to do with notions of culpability and rehabilitation?

THE JUDGE

The judge is, in common stereotypes, a semireligious figure, handing down evenhanded justice and symbolizing the majesty of the law. He is the power in the courtroom, determining the fate of the accused. He is a man whose job is, in many ways, to "play God," to pass judgment on the past and future of men's lives.

In fact, in the defendants' eyes the judge is usually a relatively peripheral figure in the criminal justice system. He is something of a figurehead, possessing power but delegating it to the prosecutor. His is among the easiest job in the system, for he takes his cues about what he ought to do from the prosecutor and acts something like a rubber stamp—stamping "legitimate and final" upon the deal that has been worked out.

What about the judge who sentenced you? Did he seem concerned about your welfare? Hostile to you? Matter of fact?

I feel that a judge really ain't shit, you know. He's just put up there—he's supposed to be the head of the show, but he ain't nothing.

Who runs the show?

The person who runs the show is the prosecutor.

Well, what's the judge's job?

The judge's job is to sit on his ass and do what the prosecutor tells him to do.

* * *

How did the judge seem? Did he seem concerned with your welfare? Hostile? Matter of fact?

No, the judge that sentenced me was like—see, the prosecutor is the fellow that gives you the time.

* * *

Well, did you get the feeling that the judge was neutral or that he was on one side or the other?

I think he was neutral. To me, man, it seemed like the judge, he up there, it don't seem like sides. You see him sitting up there like this . . . and the prosecutor and everybody—like your lawyer is talking toward the judge, but he's talking to the prosecutor; and the prosecutor is talking toward the judge, but he's talking to your lawyer, you know. That's just all, the way the thing goes.

The source of this feeling about the judge has been discussed in previous chapters. The two major appearances before the judge—the entering of the plea of guilty and sentencing—are largely rituals. When the cop-out is entered, the judge asks the defendants questions but does not seem to them particularly interested in their replies as long as they follow a certain pattern. On sentencing day he listens to the arguments of the two attorneys and, sometimes, of the defendant himself. The exercise of his discretion is typically delegated to the prosecutor, whose recommendation is usually followed. Although the judge possesses the power to refuse the recommendation, this is a fairly rare occurrence.

This is not to say that in fact the judge is without power. He may (and apparently does in some jurisdictions) participate in the deal that is recommended by the prosecutor. Moreover, even when the judge does not participate directly, anticipated reactions may influence the prosecutor's behavior in agreeing to deals. That is, the prosecutor may take into account expectations about what the judge will find acceptable in deciding what kind of deal to offer. Thus, though the two appearances before the judge may appear to the defendants to be rituals, the judge may in fact exercise more power than might be inferred from their observations of the prosecutor's recommendations and the judge's acceptance. But the defendant's perceptions are important, for they influence the lessons he learns from his encounter with criminal justice.

Why do judges behave this way? Why do they seem to abrogate their potential role as God in favor of what seems to the defendant to be a puppet for the prosecutor-ventriloquist? Why shouldn't they exercise their independent judgment, stand aloof from the politics of the system, and make decisions based upon criteria other than horse-trading and what the market will bear? Several factors were suggested by defendants to explain this rather mysterious behavior by the judge.

Perhaps, some believe, the judge defers because the prosecutor knows more about the case. The judge must hear many, many cases, they suggested, and hence must rely upon the prosecutor because the judge is not in a position to look very deeply into any particular case:

> Like [the judge] takes the prosecutor's viewpoint; sometime I see him reading from different records he have, but like the prosecutor have all the information, and the judge goes by what he says. It's his information; so the prosecutor is the judge too. Like he say, I'm giving you just so much time, you know, and the judge will say, Yeah, well, fine, he gets that much time.

*   *   *

> The prosecutor's the one who presents the case; he knows more about the defendant and everything. If he should deserve to go to jail or what. The judge never seen these people before; he don't know practically nothin about their past history or nothin. So he just takes for granted that the prosecutor knows what he's doin.

*   *   *

Do you think the judge was fair?

He was fair enough. He could have been worse.

Well, why do you think the judge didn't send you to jail?

I really don't know. Because I know he didn't have too much to do with what my lawyer and the prosecutor was doin. It's really the prosecutor—they're the ones that tell the judge what they'd like for the person to do, and the judge don't do nothin but repeat it, you know.

A lot of people say that. You know, that the prosecutor's the one that gives the time. Why do you think judges are like that? Why do they accept what the prosecutor says when presumably they could do whatever they wanted?

Well, cause really the prosecutor's the one that's studying the case. The judge don't do nothin but sit there and listen to him. And if it's the prosecutor's suggestions, Well I think this is . . . and the judge thinks it's good, then that's what it's gonna be. Like if the judge is out there and he's interested in the case too, and he's checkin out and he finds somethin different, then they can have a disagreement. But like the judge doesn't do nothin but glance through the thing. The prosecutor says, Well, I think this gentleman have a pretty bad record, and I think he should go ahead and go to jail, and that's what happens. [Judges] don't have too much time. I don't think a judge wants to sit up there and hear somebody's history or their whole life history. They just want to know what's goin on as far as the case is concerned.

It is important to recall that, though many men asserted that the prosecutor's role was preeminent because he "knew more" about the case, the same men felt that the prosecutor really didn't take much into account in deciding what sentence to recommend other than the ballpark figure. That is, in asserting that the judge lets the prosecutor take control of cases because of his greater knowledge, the men are not thereby suggesting that the prosecutor himself knows very much about the case. He decides upon a deal on the basis of bargaining and the like and recommends it to the judge. The judge, according to this theory, accepts the recommendation because the prosecutor knows more. There is a crucial gap, though, because, in the defendants' view, nobody has really looked in the first place.

Another theory suggested—somewhat less frequently—to explain the judge's abdication is his desire to avoid work.

What about the judge who sentenced you? Did he seem concerned about your welfare? Hostile? Matter of fact?

Matter of fact.

How do you think he saw his job?

I think that a lot of judges leave most of this burden of concern about what the penalty should be given the defendant up to the prosecutor.

A lot of guys say that. Why do you think they do that?

Maybe it's just—human nature. It's a way he can get out of work. He feels that the prosecutor can consider all the circumstances and in depth, and the prosecutor feels his recommendation is just. Now, I guess he gives some consideration of the defense attorney, but he knows all paid defense attorney, they being paid to say what they say, and that's just about it.

Do you think [being a judge] is a hard job?

No, it's a very easy job. It's the easiest of the three. All you have to go through—go by the rules, [and] they don't even seem to do that sometimes.

Thus, the judge can let the prosecutor have his way because it is easier that way. The response of the last man was quite common: most felt that being a judge was, in practice, rather easy. It is the position to which defense lawyers and prosecutors aspire because judges enjoy the most prestige and are paid more. At the same time, most defendants feel that under the current system it is an easy task, for the judge simply has to sit and listen and accept the pleas and the sentence recommendations.

Although most felt that it was an easy job, few said that they themselves would like to be judges. For some this response was simply a product of dislike for the legal system, of wanting to have nothing to do with it. For others fear of retaliation by the defendants they would have to sentence produced a disinclination to aspire to a judgeship. For the bulk of the men, though, being a judge was undesirable because it involved passing judgment upon the lives of others—something that most defendants felt would be an unpleasant task. Thus, most tended to distinguish between the role of the judge as they saw him in practice and the manner in which they felt he ought to behave. Most felt that the judges they encountered simply accepted lies as truth and abdicated their authority to the prosecutor.

But the defendants, when thinking of *themselves* as judges, felt that they would feel anguish and pain and a desire to inquire more deeply into each case that came before them. They clearly had a concept of what it is to be a judge much closer to that found in drama and legal theory than to what they found in the courtroom itself. This disjunction disconcerted many of them.

For a variety of reasons, then, most defendants believe that the judge is a somewhat peripheral figure, unless—on rare occasions—he has a personal bias against the defendant or an antipathy toward a given crime. This deference by the judge leads many defendants to wonder why, in fact, we bother to have judges at all.

> The judge doesn't know you. I don't really know what the judge's job is. All I know is that my lawyer went to the prosecutor and told him my story, and he came back and told me the prosecutor was going to give me the suspended. I don't even know what the judge's job is.

> * * *

> *Did [the judge] seem fair to you?*

> I saw him for about five minutes when I stood before him; so I can't make any opinion on it.

> *How do you think a judge decides on a sentence? He could have given you anything up to five years.*

> Ah, it's all planned ahead of time. At least that's the way it seems to me. It's like my lawyer came out before I changed my pleas, and he told me what they were going to give me. So it's planned some place ahead of time.

> * * *

> Well, what do you need him up there for then? What does it help being up there? He's a judge; if he's a fair judge, he's supposed to, I think he should weigh his own decision on the case. He can listen to the prosecutor or the plea—the plea of the defending attorney. But as far as just taking his recommendation at face value and just repeating it after him, he has no business there.

> * * *

Do you think [the judge] was fair?

Well, how can I say do I think *he* was fair, you know. He didn't sentence me. I was sentenced beforehand when I made the deal. See what I mean?

So in effect you're saying that you sentenced yourself?

Right. I knew what it was. When I walked in the court, I was positive in my mind that I was gettin four years. I didn't know about [the maximum]. I know it could of fluctuated, but it didn't make much difference; and I was well aware I was getting four years. I knew I'd have to go through the usual rigamarole and the judge would say certain things like this. He has to give you certain reasons for saying certain things.

Others expanded on the same theme, suggesting that if the judge behaves as he does, the sentencing process itself becomes somewhat meaningless.

Suppose you'd been the judge sitting in your case. I mean if you were a judge faced with you, how much time would you give him?

Well, I could have received twelve to twenty years, you know, and that's what I would have gave out, twelve to twenty years.

Why?

It's—you know, like—why? Why shouldn't I give him the maximum? If he brought his case before me and he's presented before a jury and he's convicted, hey, he needs the maximum.

Suppose it was you. Here's a guy, and he comes before you, and he's copped out and said, "I'm guilty."

And said, "I'm guilty"?

Yeah. Would you give him twelve to twenty?

No. Like I'd review his past record and things of that nature— review his record and look at his past history and what not and see if he deserve all this time. You know, I guess that's the way they base it.

What do you think a judge takes into account in deciding the sentence?

Your record, your school record, your work record. Well, like they have everything about you there—your personality, your attitudes, your achievements. Everything about you right there, and when he goes through all of this and then he says, Bam. Here you go out. Bye.

That's how he decided to give you a one-to-three?

No, that's not how he decided to give me a one-to-three. That was a deal that was made. As far as my record was concerned, he'd of gave me the five-to-eight, five-to-seven, and sent me on my way.

Students of the criminal justice system have also noted this consequence of the bargain justice system:

> . . . the guilty plea process, much more than the trial, encapsulates the steps immediately preceding and following conviction. Both the charging decision and sentencing merge into the conviction decision, particularly in the negotiated plea, so that concerns at this stage are not uniquely those of adjudication, of final guilt or innocence, but are intertwined with the prosecutor's discretion and the sentencing discretion of the judge. . . . The process of plea negotiation affects both the length of correctional control and the determination of who is incarcerated and who is placed on probation. To the extent that a major correctional objective is the treatment and rehabilitation of criminal offenders, the existence of plea bargaining makes the selection for major treatment alternatives and the time under correctional control a matter of skill in negotiation rather than solely a function of the treatment needs of the offender.[2]

The general view of the judge as a figurehead flies in the face of most of our presumptions about the role of the judge and is among the most significant aspects of the defendant's view of criminal justice. As we have stressed before, the system appears to the defendant to have no real neutral or principled figures in it. Everyone has a job to do and an axe to grind or is, like the judge, viewed as primarily indifferent. The determinants of the disposition of the case are largely similar to the determinants of a defendant's own behavior on the street. Short-run self-interest or indifference seems to the defendant to characterize the activities of the prosecutor and the judge. The only really "personal" characteristic of great consequence is the defendant's past criminal record. Most believe that, in the abstract at least, this criterion ought to be of relevance, but that much more ought to be taken into account. The defendants want someone to do them some good, for most are not particularly satisfied with their lives or content with the crimes they commit. At the very least, even if no one is wise enough to decide upon some treatment that will really improve him and his lot, at least someone ought to *care*, ought to agonize over the decisions that will affect the defendants' lives. As they view it, though, no one even agonizes, much less comes up with solutions to his problems. The police, the prosecutor, the public defender are all simply doing their jobs, are working under constraints placed by the production ethic that make attention to particular defendants' needs either too much work or irrelevant to their functions.

The perceived behavior of the judge is the ultimate failure of the system in their eyes. He is the one man whose job *might* involve caring and attention to the individual. He has, in their eyes, reached the pinnacle of his career, for he has attained the prestigious position that members of the legal community are thought to covet. He is fixed for life. He is, putatively, indebted to no one. Moreover, the defendants, like the rest of us, have been imbued with the myth of the judge as the independent figure—removed from petty and partisan concerns—meting out justice in some kind of evenhanded manner. He embodies the majesty and authority of the law. He embodies the principles of right conduct that the law itself is supposed to exemplify and that the defendants themselves are in many ways eager to accept.

His apparent abdication, his betrayal of authority, his willingness to appear to turn things over to just another "worker"—the prosecutor—epitomize the failure of the system in the defendants' eyes. The activities of the other actors—their lack of concern, their pressuring, conning, lying—are, to the defendants, a product of the job, something they can understand. The indifference of the judge is more difficult to swallow, for they perceive that he potentially suffers from far fewer constraints than the others. He can be *God*. If he can't necessarily straighten them out, at least he can *care*. But he doesn't. Therefore, no one does. The administration of justice is very much like the street, for no one is in fact truly disinterested or authoritative. The production ethic infects everyone, even the man who might potentially be immune to it. The irrelevance of the judge is, from the defendants' perspective, the ultimate failure of American criminal justice.

---

1. Alschuler, "The Prosecutor's Role in Plea Bargaining," pp. 54–55.

2. Donald J. Newman, *Conviction* (Boston: Little, Brown and Company, 1966), pp. 232, 238.

The Nature of Law and the Causes of Crime

The law is, among other things, a series of commands about how people in a society ought to behave. The criminal law consists of a series of negative propositions—for example, Thou shall not steal or rob or rape or murder or shoot drugs. These norms tell us what we ought not to do and at the same time—if they are obeyed —define the quality of life in our society. Some of the norms are directly tied to the economic system—for example, those protecting private property—and others are derived from basic moral notions about how people ought to treat one another. These norms not only provide a framework for social and economic life in a society but also provide a regularity and predictability to one's relations with others.

The norms that comprise the criminal law are in part the product of morality and convention among members of the society. That is, the formal doctrine is produced by notions of what is right and wrong. Norms that no longer comport with moral standards begin to fall into disuse and may become "dead-letter" laws—still on the books but not obeyed or enforced—or may be formally expunged from the criminal code. Thus, conduct conforming to the law is not only the product of a socialization process that teaches the value of obedience to law. It is also the product of unthinking moral imperatives that have no direct reference to the content of the law itself.

Most people in the society refrain from breaking into their neighbor's houses for reasons more complex than simply because they know this conduct is illegal and may produce sanctions by officers of the law; neither do most fail to steal simply because they realize that it is in their own interest for people to respect the property of others. Most also do not steal because they believe that it is *wrong* to do so.

The relationship between law, morality, and convention is two edged. In part the norms are the product of convention and morality; in part obedience to the law is itself a matter not only of the dictates of the law but also of one's own moral code.

In this chapter we shall explore the defendants' views of the law and of violation of the law. The question of why some people engage in "criminal" behavior is one that has long plagued societies and students of behavior. Many explanations and theories have been developed, none of which seem particularly fulfilling. It is too much to expect that criminals themselves—when asked, "Why did you do it?"—will provide us with ready answers to the question. They, too, are quite confused about why they behave as they do and would welcome an answer. This chapter will analyze their notions about the law and violation of it and offer an interpretation of what they had to say. The discussion is speculative. Since our system is so willing to permit defendants to "participate" in deciding how their criminal behavior ought to be punished, it seems reasonable to listen to some of their notions of why they broke the law.

What do the defendants think about the laws they violated? With the exception of a few arrested on drug charges, all the defendants believed that they had done something "wrong," that the law they violated represented a norm that was worthy of respect and that ought to be followed:

> I knew everything I did out there, it was wrong. I knew. You know, like, I was breaking the law; I knew what I was doing. I knew I wasn't supposed to do that. There was nothing they need to tell me I had to do. It's not so much that I'm so concerned about anybody else. It's just like I think that when you have a country, the thing is, it is true, if you have a country, you got to have laws to keep people from—this man work all year for his money, and you go and take it from him. Got to keep you

from doing that, you know. If you didn't, you couldn't have a country. It couldn't be run.

Like the man quoted above, about half the men interviewed (thirty-five of seventy-one) were charged with property crimes. Without exception all felt that laws against taking property from others were "good" laws and that such behavior should not be tolerated but merited punishment. They felt that the people they stole from "deserved" the property they had and that it was wrong to take it from them:

How did you feel about the people who owned the stuff you were taking?

Well, nine times out of ten I didn't know the people, you know? I didn't know the people. But I know when they came home and found their TV set was missing, well, I knew they felt bad. They're out there working all day, man, and come home and they see that their things are missin. I knew they felt pretty bad. But that didn't bother me, because I felt as though I got what I wanted. I'm satisfied. I'm only lookin out for myself, you know. Wasn't thinkin about the others.

Some guys tell me that, you know, they do B and E's or robberies, or other property crimes—that they in some sense feel like the people they are robbing don't deserve to have the stuff; so it's OK to take it. I gather you didn't feel that way?

No, I didn't feel that way. They deserved it because they worked for it. They probably worked forty, forty-eight hours a week, and most of the stuff probably wasn't even paid for. They deserved it. It wasn't that why I took it. I took it for the simple reason that I had a habit of drugs, and I knew that called for TV or the tape recorder. I knew I could sell it; so this is why I took it. But the people deserved it, oh yeah, they deserved it.

*   *   *

I don't hold any animosity whatsoever for somebody who has money. Matter of fact, I respect them for it. That they're intelligent enough to have it. And you know, if I ever do get it, I'll be happy to be in that same position, see what I mean? As I say, I respect them for it. And that's why I wouldn't want to change too much myself—because if I ever do get some money, which I intend to sometime, I would want to be in a position where I can, you know, control my destiny or whatever it is.

*   *   *

I don't feel too much of anything. Just as I say, like certain class of people, the way the system is set up, certain class of people have an—the system is set up and geared to their success and prosperity more so than others and another class—where it's geared that they should stay oppressed and it's hard to get out of it. Now, I felt it was in suburbia, these people *in a sense had the advantages of society more so than I did. But this still don't make what I did right.* You understand what I mean? I'm not trying to justify. I can't. (Emphasis added.)

These men, like almost all, admit to an envy of the property of others and to a desire to get the things that they don't have. But at the same time they are not really radicals bent upon destroying the system of private property, feeling that the rich have no "right" to possess what the poor do not. Rather, they feel that the law against stealing is justified, primarily because when they get the things they desire, they don't want someone (like themselves) to come along and take it from them. They understand the idea of reciprocity upon which the law is based.

The men interviewed have by and large "accepted" the norms implicit in the criminal law. But they have not "internalized" them. This is a somewhat subtle distinction, but I think it is crucial to understanding their relationship to the law and the reasons that they broke it. "Internalizing" a norm can be conceptualized as involving four steps: (1) acknowledging that the norm exists and understanding what behavior is prescribed or proscribed; (2) acknowledging the authoritativeness of the norm: accepting that it "ought" to be followed (such acceptance may be the product of a variety of factors: of a sense that the behavior prescribed enjoys a moral status; of an instrumental calculation that following a norm will provide benefits to the person by maintaining his property or protecting himself; of knowledge that failure to obey the norm will produce punishment that makes disobedience not worthwhile); (3) developing feelings of virtue (or self-worth) when one engages in conduct in conformity with the norm and guilt (negative feelings about oneself) when one violates the norm. (4) As a consequence of the first three steps, a norm is internalized when a person has a basic predisposition to behave in ways that are congruent with the norm. Only in extraordinary circumstances will the person consider violating the norm. In a man's day-to-day life the notion of disobeying the norm usually does not occur. Thus, internalization is a product both of a socialization process which teaches that the behavior prescribed by the norm is inherently desirable and satisfying in and of itself and of instrumental calculations that following norms will produce more personal benefit than disobedience.

Most norms violated by the men I interviewed have been internalized by most citizens in our society—at least by those who have a modicum of money and status. Most citizens, even when they are in some financial difficulty, do not consider the possibility of actually breaking into a house or robbing a liquor store; when they become angry at someone, they do not typically think seriously about beating him up or perhaps killing him; when they are anxious or despairing, they do not cop heroin and shoot up. The fact that most citizens do not think about committing these "crimes" is not simply the product of their being "crimes," nor of a fear of going to jail. They do not think of them, for they have learned that such behavior is not within the range of alternatives that they can actually consider. In part it is also the product of a Kantian imperative, a view that if everyone engaged in these acts, each man would be worse off than if no one did them. Thus, because of both socialization and calculation, most norms in the criminal law have been internalized by most people in our society.

The men I interviewed have not, by and large, internalized these norms. They have achieved the first two steps, but not the third or fourth. Difficulties encountered in their lives quickly bring to mind courses of action that involve law violation. Although they are aware of the norms and acknowledge their authoritative status, they are typically aware of and consider the possibility of violating them, and in fact do violate them with great frequency.

Some evidence of this emerged in their replies to the question, "What do you think would happen if there were no law against [the

crime that you were charged with or convicted of committing]?"
Without exception they responded, in effect, that everyone would
begin doing it. Although a few introduced some subtlety into their
response—for example, those who were richer would be less likely
to steal; some people were less prone to violence than others—most
were quite convinced that in the absence of a law, behavior now
proscribed would become rampant. This view imputes to the law
powers that, of course, it does not possess, but indicates a great faith
in the efficacy of the law.

More important, it suggests that most of the men believe that
law-abiding behavior is the product not of convention, morality, or
internalization of the norm itself, but rather of external force imposing constraints upon a person. They seem to be suggesting that
man's natural inclination is to steal and fight and kill and shoot dope.
It is clear that there is in fact something to this argument, for if there
were not such inclinations, there would be no need for laws against
such behavior. But they are saying something more than this; they
are indicating the extent to which they have not internalized the
norms of the law. They impute a morality to the law but think that
people will not behave in a lawful manner in the absence of force.

In a very real sense these men are living in a Hobbesian state of
nature, a war of all against all. Each man is subject to his own passions
and greed, and in the absence of a Leviathan, each will wreak violence
on another's person and property. They long for this Leviathan but
do not find it. In fact, they do know it exists, for they see it around
them every day; but it is not theirs.

They see a "civil" society in the middle-class and rich society in
which their lives are embedded but of which they are not members.
This distance from "civil" society accounts in part for their failure to
internalize the norms of the criminal law and for their propensity
for law-violating behavior. The norms of the law are the product of
a "they"—the middle class and rich—whose general style of life and
whose norms the defendants accept and in fact covet deeply.

We can view the defendants as spectators at a game. They see the
players; they see the rules they live by; and they envy them the opportunity to play and the rules by which the game proceeds. At the
same time, they are *not* players. The rules, therefore, are not theirs.
They are involved in another game, and the rules of civil society do

not serve their interests—they serve the interests of the members of that society. Thus, they have not internalized the rules—the thought and the practice of violating them occur to them frequently—even though they recognize them and accept them as desirable guides to life. Let us look now at the defendants' views of the causes of crime. It is useful to distinguish between those who were drug addicts at the time of their last arrest and those who were not.

THE JUNKIE

About half the men interviewed reported that they had been using heroin at the time of their last arrest.* It is difficult to tell whether this is an accurate reflection of the proportion of those who commit crimes in Connecticut. The men in prison were selected randomly, and the estimate of prison officials suggests that 50 percent is probably reasonably accurate.

The drug addicts—who were in prison for drug offenses or property crimes, most frequently breaking and entering—reported that they had committed their crimes for the purpose of obtaining money to support their drug habits, which ranged from about eighteen to one hundred dollars a day. Thus, for these men the real question seems to be not why they committed crimes, but rather why they became drug addicts. It may not be that simple, for I have the impression that many of them might well have been involved in criminal activities even if they had not been addicted. Many had criminal records that preceded their experience with drugs. Moreover, a number of men interviewed had been drug addicts in the past but apparently had not been addicts at the time of their last arrest.

Why does a man become a drug addict? Most of the men who were addicts had theories, though none really thought they completely understood their behavior or the general phenomenon. Most suggested that their initial experience had to do with watching people around them apparently quite happy on drugs and being curious about what it was like. This led to experimentation, to enjoyment, to

---

* Thirty-seven of seventy-one reported that they were heroin users at the time of their last arrest. Thirty-one reported that they were addicted to heroin.

habitual use, and to addiction. Others spoke of the notion of "escape," of being in a position in which nothing could bother them, in which life became tolerable. Others talked of the status attached to use of drugs; others of psychological weakness and the need for a crutch. All agreed that heroin was enjoyable, though supporting a habit was not:

What kind of person would be an addict, and what kind of person wouldn't?

What kind of person? Anybody can get hooked—anybody can get hooked. You can be around the wrong crowd; you could have your best friends, they'll get you hooked. Anybody—your wife, your girlfriend; maybe your mother and your father, your uncle and your aunt. Anybody can get you hooked. You bein around it so much, that's what it is now. There's so much in the street—all your friends are doin it—you can't help from getting around it. It's in the ghettos, it's in the suburbs. You can't help from gettin around it. In the ghetto there is nothin to do, really, nothin to do but shoot pool. Maybe go to a party or a dance, that's it. We don't bowl, we don't swim; so you get tired of liquor. You know, when you're young, you get a lot of wine— muscatel, Thunderbird, Gypsy Rose—all that fade away. You graduate gradually. Now you about thirteen, fifteen, sixteen, you in the pool room shootin pool—BAM! Dude is here sellin dope. Got a big bankroll in his pocket. So he say, "Try a snuff, man." So, man, this is out of sight—BAM! It relaxes your nerves. You don't care about nobody—and don't nobody pay any attention to you. When you got it, you real friendly and everything. It just calms you down automatically.

*   *   *

Curiosity. There's a lot of things—curiosity, problems—a lot of things, you know, that lead a person falling into the cooker. More people are trying to solve—no, not trying to solve, but they're trying to escape the reality of their problems by getting into their cooker. And where they used to fall into the liquor bottle, well, they're not fallin into the liquor bottle anymore. They're falling into the heroin cooker.

Why?

Well, like this—I don't know; I can't say. I used drugs because, you know, like problems—well, I can face [them], but there's just something that I like to do, you know?

You just enjoy it?

Right. But, now, some of my friends—well they use drugs because they have problems, and they're trying to hide from them. But as long as they hide, they can forget their problems. But as soon as they come down, the problem's still there. So actually they didn't solve anything. They've got a bigger problem then, when they get a habit.

*   *   *

Why do you suppose most people start using heroin?

Out of curiosity—you know? Just bein curious. Like I started just wantin to know what it was like, and then once you find out what it's like, really, you involved. You can't just pull away from it.

A lot of people say it's fun.

From the beginning it's fun. Once you get a habit, it's not fun no more, you know. Now, a lot of people come to jail and kick their habit, go back on the street again. They kicked the habit physically, but mentally they still have the shootin the drugs in their mind, you know.

Why do they go back? Because they like it?

Well, not because they like it. Well, that could be a part of it too—because they like it—that could be a great part of it too. But nine out of ten of 'em go back to it because they need the feeling; they dig the feeling of the high. And most likely live in an environment where most people use it. Maybe half of their associates use it, you understand? So they have no choice: either run away from the problem or stay there and try to fight it. If you stay and try to fight it, you're not gonna win, because you don't have very much will power, I don't think. A person that never experienced that, can't, you know, say nothin about it— what it do to you or what it don't do to you. Because when you sick, then junk is best, really, the very best. But we start out usin it from curiosity, want to see what it's like. We see this fellow

noddin, meditatin, you know. Say, "Man, you look pretty nice";
man, he's high. So you try it. It feel nice. You don't get no habit
the first time you try it, you know; so you try it again, and then
you start doin it every day, like high every day. Then after two
weeks, three weeks, your back starts hurtin when you get up in
the mornin. Then you go get you some stuff—you feel pretty
nice now. After two months, man, you strung out. You got to
have it, got to have it. Before, you had to have it, but now you
got to have it or you suffer.

*   *   *

If you're in a good frame of mind, heroin is not that enjoyable.
But if you're depressed—when I started using it, I was coming
out of a really bad crisis in my life, and so, you know, it enabled
me to forget about it. It gave me something to do more than
anything [else]. I'd get up in the morning and I'd say, "Well, I
got something to do today. I got to get the money together. I
got to cop without getting caught. I got to make sure it's good
stuff, and I got to get off." And then I would worry about what
I'm going to do for pleasure after that. And it was that as much
as [it was] the sensation of being high—it was a lifestyle.

Thus, a man gradually was drawn into addiction. With his addiction went a good deal of criminal activity since habits can cost a
lot of money. Some sold drugs to support their habits; others concentrated on "boosting" (shoplifting) or breaking and entering. Their
lives had a Sisyphean quality, for success in copping dope and getting
off was simply a prelude to further search for money to get more
drugs. Most seemed to hate their lives as addicts, for they were on a
treadmill. But their attitudes toward heroin were more than a little
equivocal. Most felt that it was a "bad" drug; it destroyed lives. But
many—as the third man quoted above—seemed in their discussion of
their experience as junkies to be arguing with themselves as much as
they were describing their past experience. They didn't want to go
back to drugs, but then again they did.

What would you like to be doing [ten years from today]?

Have my family. Have a nice home. Shoot all the drugs I want
to. Just make me happy; all I want to do is be happy. I want to
be just like anybody else. I want to bowl, I want to fish. But I

don't have time for it, because I'm chasing that bag, tryin to get that cash to get that bag.

What do you think you'll be doing in ten years?

Wish I could predict the future, but—the way things are now, sometimes—like now—I got the urge for some drugs. Somebody drop a bag of it, I probably would shoot it. That's the way it is. No use to beatin around the bush. I'm tellin you how I feel inside. I'm a for real person, and I'm tellin you for real how I feel. And most drug addicts feel the same way. Anytime I get in a conversation with 'em, they talk about it.

This man, and many like him, will probably return to drugs when released from prison. He will then continue to commit a variety of crimes to support his habit. Much of his crime will go undetected, but eventually he will be caught and will return to prison.

Why does he do it? The roots of his behavior lie both within himself and within the social system in which he lives. Clearly, drugs serve some basic need for this man and for most addicts. He desires gratification of his desire to "be happy" or to forget "his problems," and he wants it fast. This man, and most of the other addicts, seem to share a lack of self-control, a tendency to see the world as something beyond their control. In a very real social and economic sense, this is a correct view, for the world offers them few opportunities to get jobs or live lives that have meaning or a future. Moreover, they see themselves as somewhat out of their own control. A common theme expressed by drug addicts was a fear of man's impulses, a notion that he is subject to passions that he cannot control. The addictive quality of heroin produces a kind of physiological equivalent of this psychological feeling of being at the mercy of others' and of one's own impulses. In this sense heroin addiction, for many, may be functional, for it produces external structure to lives that comports with the individual's own image of himself and place in society.

CRIMINALS WITHOUT HABITS

The remainder of the men interviewed were not acting out of the compulsion to obtain drugs that motivated the dope addict. Their crimes, which included breaking and entering, robbery, weapons charges, and assaults, were committed for other reasons: they wanted goods or money; they were angry with someone and punished them or sometimes killed them. Some of their crimes were calculated; some were done in the heat of anger. Many expressed a desire for gratification quickly rather than in the future:

> There was things I wanted and—it's not because I'm too lazy to work for 'em. The things I wanted just seems too far off and pretty hard to—just like a new car and nice clothes, and maybe some day I wanted maybe a nice house and stuff. I was lookin ahead of the future. I know just working take twenty years, ten years to get these things, and I got caught up with my own thoughts, got all messed up, got myself all involved, and that's it. As I was fifteen to sixteen years [old], seemed like everybody else had cars. I didn't, you know. I wanted a car and things like this. I felt, boy, how am I gonna work and save a thousand dollars and another five hundred dollars for insurance. Boy, by the time I do this, then I'll be an old man. Really you're not, but this is the way you think.

This is a common theme offered by the men who committed property crimes: they wanted things, and they didn't see how they could get them soon enough by working at jobs; so they "had" to turn to crime.[1] Thus, crime is a method of obtaining material things for these men, and for many a method that seems simpler than a job:

> Well, like now as far as the employment thing goes, like you have to be a mastermind to get the type of job you want. Like you gotta not only be a high school grad, but you have to specialize in a certain field to get what you want. And people are getting tired of that. Everybody don't have the ability to go to school, or they don't have the patience to go to school and take the time to get these degrees and what not; so they learn somethin in the meantime. They learn how to steal, or they learn how to play card games. There's a thousand and one things that you do. Like I learned how to play all these games. You learn how to do 'em because they're easier—aw, no, now I wouldn't—hell, no, they're not easier, not by a long shot. Everything that I can do wrong, it's not easier than being on a job, you know? I'd

rather have that eight hours, but it's just that that eight hours would—like the $200 I may get for working that week, you know, I may have $1,600 for that same forty hours; so why should I throw $1,400 away for $200? It's not easier, but it's more profit. No, it's not easier, but it's more profitable. Wrong is more profitable.

Do you think that's why more and more people are violating the law?

Oh, yes and no. Yes, they violate the laws to get the money, yes. No, they violate the laws because they have to, you know? Some dudes, they try, try, try everything. They're not suited for any of these; so they get disgusted. They're not making no money; so they try something different. He may have a rusty old pistol thrown up in the drawer somewhere, you know, and he see that his shoe is getting sort of low, and the seat of his pants gettin sort of thin, and his shirt don't look too fine no more. So he decides, well, now you see that old pistol over there in that drawer. He goes and gets that pistol and looks at it and says, "Roscoe, we going out and get us some squares tonight." You know? And he goes out and sticks up some joint. He never did it before, no, but he's gotten away with the money; so he got away with it the one time. That may be three hundred dollars, yeah. It may last him a couple of days cause fast money goes fast. The faster it comes, the faster it leaves. Yeah, yeah, you can't save it too tough. Naw, you can't save it too tough. It's hard, it's very hard to save. But, anyway, he start with a three-hundred-dollar stick-up, maybe a liquor store. Right? And he keeps climbin the scale. He's not gonna keep on robbin these liquor stores for three hundred dollars. Then he go to a loan company and get three thousand. Not going to go to the loan company no more if he can go to a bank and get $3 million, you know? He keeps progressin. With a little thought you can do anything and get away with it.

*　　*　　*

All the prices on everything is all gettin higher, and stuff like that.

People are stealing just to support themselves?

A lot, yeah. I did for a long time.

Why do people do that instead of getting a job?

It's hard to find jobs now. Hell, it's damn hard to find jobs. Cause I was out there for four months. I couldn't find a job. One job last me a week, and I got fired for not goin in. That was my fault, but I had real bad hours, was only gettin $1.80 an hour.

*   *   *

Why do you suppose most people break the law against B and E?

To get money, furniture—mostly just money.

Why do you suppose some people get money that way and some people have jobs? What do you think differentiates the people who break and enter from the people who don't?

It's easier work to break into a place than working eight hours and forty hours a week. Break into a place—there half an hour, and you make almost as much pay.

*   *   *

Probably everything in general. There's more people than ever. Cities are bigger. Narcotics are widespread. Keeping up with the Joneses. Everything is more or less geared to material things, personal material things—cars, clothes, etc. And everything is higher now. In the past maybe a man was content to have a mule and forty acres. Now it's a car and maybe a couple of suits.

These men express two common themes: the material gain that criminal behavior can produce and an unwillingness or inability to make similar gains by noncriminal behavior. The notion that crime pays was expressed by many of the men; but very few believe, as the first man quoted suggests, that one can indefinitely get away with crimes. In the long run the "small-time" criminal will always be caught. But he can get away with a lot before the day of reckoning:

When you do a B and E, nobody sees you. And although they have a good idea who did it, it's very hard unless the person you're with testifies against you in order for you to get convicted, or they catch you red-handed first. As I say, I've been arrested and actually sent to jail three times on breaking and entering.

And when they arrested me, I might give them another five or six that they knew I did. But how many—maybe I've done fifty or seventy-five that, you know, they couldn't ever convict me on. See, the time is very minimal as far as the crime goes, and you can still get a lot of breaking and entering, and it's very hard to catch you on one.

This man suggests the calculation that many go in for: comparing the rewards of working with the gains that may acrue from illegal behavior. Several characteristics of the calculation stand out. First, most assume that for any given job they will not be caught, though in the long run they will. Second, the payoff is seen as typically greater than could be obtained by other, noncriminal activity. This is both a result of distaste for the types of jobs that are available and for the deferment of gratification that working for a living typically entails. Finally, the price that must be paid for failure—for getting caught—is not perceived as too high to warrant the risk involved. This last feeling results from both a self-deception—the denial that they *will* get caught—and from the fact—that prison simply isn't so *bad*. For the younger men who have not been there before, it even holds some mystery and excitement. For the older men who have already done time, it is something they feel that they can "handle." For both, though, the crucial factor is that life on the street is not so good. None of the men wanted to be in prison, for they enjoy freedom and the ability to attempt to meet their needs—for which freedom is essential. But neither is life on the street such a lark either, for it too involves a good deal of frustration in attempting to fulfill their wants. Thus, for the junkie and the nonjunkie, prison is not—relative to life on the street—sufficiently undesirable. At the same time, it does not strike me that making prison conditions harsher or lengthening sentences would solve this difficulty. First, the defendants typically—as suggested before—tend to convince themselves that they will not get caught for any one crime. The "rational" man would probably conclude that the odds of being caught for the typical B&E are quite slight; the defendants imagine the odds as even more in their favor. Moreover, even an extended stay in prison may not be an effective deterrent so long as life on the street is not itself especially desirable.

Another common explanation for crime offered by the defendants

—particularly for property crimes—suggested that there was a kind of excitement and satisfaction in getting away with it. Sometimes this view simply seemed to reflect a child's delight in putting something over on his parents; for other men it suggested more: an alienation from the forces of law and order. It was also, for some, the emotional thrill or sense of accomplishment in doing something that is highly dangerous—in a sense "crime" is like auto racing, mountain climbing, or skydiving. It is difficult to sort these out and more difficult to understand exactly what kind of excitement the men found in the crime, for they were often unable to describe it in detail:

I didn't need the money in a sense, but I went in there mainly for the money—but I didn't need it, have to have it. I wasn't doing drugs like the rest of my friends. It was so easy. I can't explain it. I know I'm not crazy, cause I got good sense. But it's just that first day—all it took was people weren't home, open the window, crawled in. It was just like that, that easy, and it was open. I was scared plus excited at the same time.

What about the other times? Same way?

The same way, but you get less scared.

*   *   *

Well, sure, there's a satisfaction out of it. It's almost like when you're winning at games—you were a sports fanatic, which I am too, you know, something like that. But I can't even say that, when I was doing these things, I got more satisfaction out of that than actually out of the money. Because I've never had trouble with money, you know. I was always a fairly good gambler when I was a kid and everything. I didn't need money that badly.

What was the satisfaction?

Just like winning. You know, maybe you were rebelling a little bit; I don't say it was that strong—I wasn't just doing it for that alone, you know.

If it was a game, who was the opponent?

Well, to tell the truth, I'm thinking now I could pull all kinds of ideas from my mind who the opponent would be. Back then I wouldn't, you know, couldn't really define anything like that.

What would you say now?

Well, I'd say that I was trying to beat the police—something like that. But I think that really is—if you were to think about that—it really is just an excuse for the many reasons for doing it.

*   *   *

Did you ever think you might get sent to prison?

I didn't think that I was gonna ever get caught.

Why not?

Because I had a style. There's a style to selling drugs. And if it wasn't for a friend of mine, the informer, I wouldn't be here now. I'd still be out there selling drugs. Yeah. There's a style.

You thought you were so good at it that they wouldn't get you?

That's right. And apparently I was, you know, until he [the friend-turned-informer] got mad with me and brought two agents to me. Because as far as the blue coat was concerned, he could never touch me. They tried many a time, but they could never do anything to me. Take me to the police station, shake me down; the lieutenant say, "Let him go, he's clean." Yeah. I look at him and laugh. Make an ass of him on the way back to the street. You know? They do that. Yeah.

Why?

Why? Because I knew that he knew that I was doing wrong, but he couldn't prove it. He never had no proof. When I got arrested, they had a stack of statements this high, you know, about me and my activities, but maybe that's only hearsay, you know. You can't take me into court and convict me nowheres in the country on that hearsay. I don't know nothing about this; so I laughed. It made me feel good to know that they put up enough time and effort to try and catch me and they couldn't, they couldn't.

Why did it make you feel good?

It made me feel good to know that I was doing something and getting away with it. Yeah. Yes, that's what made me feel all right.

*   *   *

It's a strange experience—breaking into something. Your body is just sort of caterpillars running through it, and you get these strange feelings.

Is it enjoyable?

Ah, it was.

Exciting?

It was. There was no reason for me to go out and do it. I just went out and did it. I can't justify my reason. I didn't need the money that bad to go out and break into places. Ah, I just did it. I had fun doing it.

*   *   *

I do things like that, you know, to get back even for, you know?

Who are you getting back at?

Really you're not gettin back at nobody but yourself, you know.

Who do you feel like you're getting back at?

Like on the people—you outslicked em, you know?

"Them" is the cops?

The—you know, yeah—the law. All right, so I was out there, right? See, the man, he's not lookin at me, you know? I'm getting by, and it makes you feel good. You're thinking maybe, I can do things. Or if you just do it because you're just completely lost. You want a piece, you know; you think you're bein somebody.

*   *   *

Did you ever think about getting caught?

Yeah. I knew I'd get caught sooner or later.

You thought you would be caught?

Sooner or later. Well, I played the game to see how long I could stay up. Just like anybody. Boy, if you could get a rerun. I wish I had a video tape in my pocket to show you how hard it was for them to catch me. You'd roll in the floor laughing of all the stuff I did to get away. They only took 'em two weeks to catch me, but they had to go through hell to catch me in two weeks. Runnin through swamps, swimmin, and everything to catch me, and it was really bad. And it's the truth—I'm not tryin to make it sound like a brag—"Hey, they can't catch me; I'm too good for them"—but it's the truth. I mean they so much as went and told the officer that brought me in to have an extra two-week vacation. That's how much they wanted me.

Some of the men quoted above—the last two—were young (eighteen and seventeen years old), and the "kid stuff" quality of their remarks is understandable. The others, though, were both older (from twenty to twenty-six) and generally more mature. Still, there is the quality of a child's satisfaction in their remarks. In part it is the child's satisfaction in simply getting away with something, the knowledge of doing wrong without detection or sanction. These remarks also have the quality of one who seeks *attention* from his parent by doing wrong. Although they speak of the satisfaction in terms of their not being "noticed," one gets the feeling that what they really want is just the opposite. Their satisfaction seems similar to thumbing one's nose at a powerful authority figure. The satisfaction derives not only from demonstrating that you yourself are powerful and autonomous, but also from getting the attention of your "superior," making him acknowledge your existence and care about you.

Also implicit in these remarks is a set of subcultural norms that are significantly different from those suggested by the criminal code. Stealing a car or getting away with a B and E is satisfying not only because you "get away with something" but also because it indicates that you are a tough guy, a man who has been around. Even going to prison can bring some prestige to a person—as he sees his relations with his peers—and hence is not by any means an unequivocally unpleasant or bad fate. But though there is a strain of such thought expressed by these men, it is not accurate to suggest that they are simply members of another "culture," following a fairly detailed and authoritative set of norms that are at variance with the norms of society at large. Rather, they exist within a society with norms that they accept as authoritative, yet consistently violate. They long to be able to live by these norms, yet do not.

Why, if they long for these norms, do they break them so often? In part their failure to obey them stems from the fact that the norms prescribe ways of living with one another (e.g., do not steal from your neighbor; settle your disputes by discussion or, if necessary, by recourse to the legal process) which do not fit their circumstances. One is content not to steal from his neighbor, or to settle disputes without direct violence, if these ways of living serve his interests in a reasonably effective manner. One is less likely to steal if he has other ways of making a living; he will discuss things or, if necessary, call into play legal machinery if he has a reasonable expectation that he will get some satisfaction. In many ways the men interviewed do not enjoy such alternatives.

Their short time perspective is not simply the product of personal weaknesses. It is also a product of living in a society in which the material affluence they desire is *already available* to many others in a visible way. The impatience of the defendants to get things for themselves and to get them quickly, then, is the product in part of literally being able to see and feel and taste the material satisfactions that they desire.

See, sometime I don't know what I do. Sometime I drink to make me happy; sometime I drink for things I been thinking, you know. Sometime I drink just to think, I would like to do this; I would like to do that, you know. I would like to help the people out. I would like to do the best I can. I wish I can become somebody some day. I would like to be—a man I really want to become, you know? I'm a man, but not the man I want to become. And sometime when I drink, it make me happy; sometime when I drink, it make me think. Sometime when I drink it make me do things I don't want to do. It just—things I don't want to do. Then I want to see if I can help myself, which is not good at all, because if you got a store, and I see that you got enough money—you work for that—you won't like me to go there and take your store and get the money out, you know, and get lost, because then you're gonna feel sorry. Like I've been doing myself, you know. Most of the times I've been caught for, I get on probations. Sometime I get off free. But when I do those kind of things, I feel sorry for myself. I

say to myself, Why did I doing this for? Why? How come I'm
this kind of person? I don't like to do this. I say to myself, I
wish I wasn't this kind of person I am. I want to change my
life. I want to be somebody else. I want to be a different person
than what I am. I don't like to do this to nobody. I hate to do
this to the people. And sometime I think a lot of time, How
come I see everybody—a lot of people with nice, nice things
—nice clothes, nice shoes, nice car, good job, money all the
time in the pocket. Why can I not have the same what they
got? And that make me—when I think about those—that's when
it come inside me: I want to be that kind of person; I want to
have what he got. And that's what'll make me do what I want to
get [it]. I say to myself, Just working I'm not gonna get what
I want right away. If I work, I got to wait a long time to get
what I want, and if I don't work and I do this, I might get it
fast. And then I say, But I don't like to do this, no matter how.
If I got a job and maybe it take a little time to get what I want,
but I can get it, you know?

These remarks capture, I think, the personal and social dilemmas
facing the typical defendant. He is the subject of norms prescribing
how he ought to live that emanate from the middle-class society in
which his own poverty-ridden life is embedded. He sees around him
the things that he wants, and he longs to have them. He wants them
fast because they seem so accessible. He feels himself captured by his
own wants and behaves in ways that he knows are wrong. He comes
to despise himself, to think that he is weak and a "bad man"—per-
sonalizing his guilt rather than attributing it to the social conditions
that may have caused his poverty or violence.

When he does get caught, and "they" punish him, he discovers
that they really don't care very much about him. He is a nuisance,
and they treat him as though they would some incidental bother distracting them from going about their lives. His interaction with
the law—in which he finds himself an object in the hands of those
who simply wish to get rid of him—enforces his own image of himself as an outsider and as a "bad person."

The moral ways of living that the law symbolizes and that he
himself longs for seem to have no place in the enforcement of the

law. He does not learn that those rules he violated are "right," for he knows this already; he does not learn that the more "civil" ways of treating people that the law symbolizes are available to *him*, for he is not treated in a particularly civil manner. All he really learns is that he ought to be slick, that he ought to try not to make mistakes and not get caught next time. He longs for some personal attention, for someone to "fix him up" and make him capable of living the way he wants to live, but he does not find it in the legal system. What he finds is an extension of his own life on the street, an extension of the life he hates.

In this sense the criminal justice system basically serves the function of a tax on the lives of the people who encounter it. The nature of their lives is such that they often engage in a mode of behavior—fighting, stealing, taking dope—that violates the law, for such behavior is a defining characteristic of their way of coping with their lives. The society says to them that if they do so, they will have to pay a tax to the commonweal in return for their "opportunity" to engage in such activity. Middle-class and wealthy people also have to pay taxes in return for their ability to make money, raise their families, have fun. Society values their activities (is, in fact, defined by them), and hence their tax can be paid in money. The defendants cannot pay their tax in money; so they pay it in inconvenience, pain, and sometimes loss of freedom for substantial periods of time.

The nature of our society—the fact that "we" cherish a modicum of privacy and protection of citizens against the imposition of governmental power—means that the "tax" we impose on the criminal is not so onerous that he will not be willing to pay it. Moreover, even if the tax were imposed at a much steeper rate, the relative lack of other more palatable alternatives might still make him willing to pay. So the defendant pays his tax: he lives in fear of the police, is arrested periodically, spends some time in jail, and sometimes has to go to prison. His encounters with the law are the product of his own needs and of his failure to internalize the norms of the law because they do not serve his own interests very well. His encounters with the law do not teach him moral lessons about how he ought to behave; rather, they reinforce his image of himself as an outsider, as an appendage of the society of which he would so much like to be a member.

---

1. For a discussion of the concept of time perspective as a factor in criminal behavior, see Edward Banfield, *The Unheavenly City* (Boston: Little, Brown and Company, 1970), Chapter 8.

7

The Defendant's Perspective: Some Implications

We have now concluded our survey of defendants' views of the nature of American criminal justice. Several themes have recurred: the defendant sees himself as an object in the hands of a "they" that really doesn't care very deeply about *him*; he sees in the substance of the law itself a set of principles for behavior whose morality and virtue he accepts; in the enforcement of the law he sees not principles but work—a variety of men doing their jobs; his general view of society is that of a spectator looking in and wishing he could participate in the game; his experience with the legal system confirms his status; the legal system is, in many ways, but an extension of his life on the street.

These perceptions of the operation of the legal system are not simply the fantasies of men attempting to portray their tormentors as evil or indifferent men. The image of criminal justice as an assembly line comports quite well with what other more neutral observers have to say. Moreover, the men are not in fact particularly bitter—they do not rail about the injustice that has been wreaked upon them. Rather, they are confused and somewhat disappointed. They want to be different kinds of men, and wish someone would help them attain this goal, though they do not find such assistance in their encounters with criminal justice.

The roots of their "antisocial" behavior lie in the social and economic conditions in which their lives are embedded. Whether they are junkies or not, their crimes are instrumental acts designed to achieve goals. They are also calculated, for most defendants know what they are about to do is against the law and that if caught, they will suffer punishment. The junkie probably doesn't care very much; the criminal without a habit does care, but he chooses to commit the crime anyway.

There is a growing strain of thought in this country suggesting that many "crimes" are in fact political acts, perhaps votes of no confidence in a system in which the criminal perceives that he has no other way of casting a vote. The studies of urban riots are a special case of this stream of thought, for "criminal" acts such as stealing and burning do appear to have some political significance for those who participate in riots. A phrase scrawled on sidewalks—"Theft is the obligation of the poor"—is another manifestation of this "politicization" of deviance. The counterculture's propensity for "ripping off" institutions of the establishment and for characterizing their thievery and fraud as revolutionary acts is another indication of this notion of crime.

What of the men discussed here, the "run-of-the-mill" criminals? Were their crimes "political" acts? This is a hard question to answer, for the term "political" is very slippery. In the most general notion of politics—the distribution of costs and benefits, the determination of who gets what when and how—a property crime is clearly "political" since it involves an individual act of expropriation. Clearly, too, the roots of much of the criminal behavior committed by these men lay in part at least in their economic and social condition. On the other hand, if intention is to be a guide, it is clear that the men I spoke with did not *intend* their crimes to have political or other-directed significance. They were acts—whether they involved stealing money or a car or beating someone up or selling narcotics—whose purpose was designed to attain some personal goal. Most of the men were untroubled by whom they stole from or what the consequences of their acts for the society at large might be.

More difficult is the question of whether the men—by their crimes—were implicitly "voting" no confidence in the American economic and political systems. I have tried to argue that in a very real sense they were, for I believe that one of the major reasons they committed crimes was that they did not perceive that alternative modes of more "law-abiding" behavior would suit their needs. The "rules of the game" for middle-class and wealthy society do not offer them viable alternatives, and hence they break them frequently. By the same token, though, I do not argue that their acts constitute for them an *attack* on the status quo, a cry for differing economic and political relationships, a desire for "revolution." The "revolution" that these men wish does not involve destroying American economic and political institutions. Rather, they desire a much more modest goal—the ability to participate in economic and social life, the ability to get rich, to be influential and respected. Thus, theft for them is not really an attack on the notion of private property; the B&E men—even those who are not addicts—are not naive or unrealizing "communists" attacking the capitalist system. They are men who want to enjoy the material benefits that our society offers. Far from despising material wealth, the men desire it desperately.

One can introduce a "false consciousness" argument and suggest that the very things that these men want are not in their interests, or that they really only *think* they want them. But this is, I believe, a gross distortion of how they themselves understand their behavior and how others may understand it. These men seem to want what they see others as having: houses, cars, clothes, money in their pockets. Their objection to economic and political institutions is not based upon their inherent characteristics, but upon the ways in which they seem to be working. In fact, the men cherish notions of private property and even capitalism, for they see these as essential to their eventual success in making good and distinguishing themselves. Some observers may argue that the men simply do not understand the exploitative nature of capitalism and the racism inherent in American society. Perhaps they are right, but to attempt to characterize the conduct of the men interviewed as consciously (or even implicitly) expressing such notions is a serious misunderstanding.

If it is a mistake to view the acts of the defendant as political in intent, it is equally true that crime and criminal justice are themselves integral parts of American political life. They always were. Today, the treatment of criminals has become an open issue for political dispute, with some attacking crime in the streets and the extension of procedural protections to defendants, and others decrying the erosion of due process values.

It seems clear from the defendants' perspective that the problems of criminal justice do not revolve around the overemphasis of due process values. These values imply a concern for the individual; in his encounter with criminal justice, this is precisely what the defendant does not think he finds. The objectification of individuals that is inherent in the system as it operates contradicts the "due process" model of criminal justice. How, then, should the system treat those who become enmeshed in it? Would more attention to due process concerns—to protecting the rights of the defendant, to formalizing and "judicializing" the process instead of concentrating upon the informal processes of bargaining—make things different for the defendant?

To begin with, as suggested before, simply changing the administration of American justice without also modifying the basic conditions of economic and social life for many of the poor in this country would not produce a great decrease in the incidence of criminal behavior. As long as crime appears to "pay" in the eyes of the defendants, it will probably exist. Nor does a highly Draconian system seem either feasible or desirable. It is not feasible, because our society will probably never be willing to invest in the resources for law enforcement necessary to make it possible for all or even most "crimes" to be detected and the culprits apprehended. Moreover, unless life on the streets is more attractive, crime will continue to pay even if the risks of getting caught are greatly increased.

If we cannot and do not wish to "solve" the problems of crime through a Big Brother system of law enforcement, what does the defendant's perspective suggest about other alternatives? One of the themes that I have emphasized here is that the defendant's experience with criminal justice ought in some sense to be a "lesson." It ought to teach the defendant not only that what he has done is wrong, but also that there are alternative ways in which he might live his life. It ought not be a lesson that he is an irremediably "bad" man, nor that no one in the society really knows or cares what happens to him as long as he can be gotten rid of for the moment.

I have argued that their perceived inability to participate in the society is tied intimately to their law-violating behavior. They believe in the authority of the law, but do not conform to it—at least in part because such behavior does not seem to serve their interests. The criminal justice system itself cannot make law-abiding behavior serve their interests, for economic and social forces are much more influential. But it can and should do more than simply shunt the defendant off to prison or probation, without much attention to him or his problem. It can and should indicate to him that he is not an outsider but a valuable human being. One of the most striking impressions one gets in prison is the enormous number of people (not only prisoners, but also guards and administrators) who seem to be looking for someone to talk to. The prisoners especially want to talk to someone, for they are seeking some recognition that they are men and that someone cares about them. Simply caring about a man will clearly not make him have better control of his temper or make him not think about stealing when he needs money or make him break his addiction to heroin. But openly caring about a man—looking at him as an individual rather than as an object, talking with him, showing some interest and sympathy for his own concerns and difficulties—is a start toward giving him some hope that he *might* become different. This is what I mean by the capacity for teaching a defendant a lesson, even if it is of the most rudimentary sort. Showing him that you are interested in him and are trying to do something to aid him in solving his difficulties would seem the very least that a system of criminal justice devoted to "rehabilitation" could do. But it does not even do this.

John Griffiths has recently suggested a similar point. He suggests that the criminal justice system might be restructured on the model of a family, in which the offender is treated not as an outsider or object, but rather as a kind of wayward son, whose misconduct produces punishment but not rejection. He also argues that the system ought to teach defendants lessons about right conduct by the procedures that it follows:

> Children, defendants, and everyone else, learn both from the *objective* of a process they participate in and from the *nature* of

the process. Robert Dreeben has recently written about the pedagogical effects of the structure of a schooling environment, as distinguished from the effects of the instructional content of the school's curriculum. . . . His thesis, with "defendant" substituted for "pupil" and "the criminal process" for "teachers" . . . , is precisely what is central to the Family Model conception of the relation of process to substantive functions in criminal procedure:

> Whatever pupils learn from the didactic efforts of teachers, they also learn something from their participation in a social setting some of whose structural characteristics have been briefly identified. Implicit in this statement are the following assumptions: (a) the tasks, constraints, and opportunities available within social settings vary with the structural properties of these settings; (b) individuals who participate in them derive principles of conduct based on their experiences coping with those tasks, constraints, and opportunities; and (c) the content of the principles learned varies with the nature of the setting. To the question of what is learned in school, only a hypothetical answer can be offered at this point: pupils learn to accept social norms, or principles of conduct and to act according to them.[1]

If this argument is correct—and I believe it is—it means that defendants learn lessons from their experience with criminal justice. The lessons they learn seem to suggest that life *is* a jungle, that people do not care about them, that exploitation and resource application is the way in which life is and must be lived, that those who have less lose.

Many will argue with the thesis that the system ought to be teaching different lessons. Some object that the thesis suggests that we ought—through various institutions, including those administering justice—to attempt to integrate people into an economic and social system that is itself corrupt—rotten with racism and inequality. Others have suggested to me that to attempt to teach defendants different ways to live will simply raise false expectations: they will, after their encounter with criminal justice, return to a life that is full of misery and poverty. Rather, they say, it should operate as it currently does, mirroring the exploitation and *Realpolitik* of the streets, for this is the world in which the defendants must live anyway.

Both these arguments have an appeal, but neither of them is compelling. The first suggests that it is not in the long-range interests of the defendants to be able to participate in our "civil" society, because it is a bad society. It suggests that reforms in criminal justice are a form of meliorism, simply putting off the basic structural reforms that are necessary in American society. It posits for the defendant a false consciousness of what he *ought* to desire, and suggests that the material well-being that he so covets is not what he ought to want. As I suggested above the defendant in fact *does* want to be a "good" American, to work at a job that produces a substantial income, to raise his family and send his kids to school, and so forth. To say that it is *really* in his interest to live a different kind of life is, clearly, to presume much. Moreover, it is to treat him as the criminal justice system itself treats him—as an object—making him the cannon fodder for the revolution that increasing numbers of people are coming to believe is necessary in this country. Perhaps those calling for revolution are right, but there is something extremely distasteful about denying some measure of short-run comfort to men whose lives are already so miserable, and doing so in the name of some overarching goal in which these men have little interest.

The other argument—that the criminal justice system ought to reflect life as the defendants know it—seems also to have merit. As I have suggested several times, changes in the administration of justice —in the absence of change in income distribution—would probably make little difference in the incidence of "crime." But if we are going to begin to attack the causes of "crime," then we must attack (if not begin with) problems of the administration of justice. If we are to create a society in which all citizens are to be treated with dignity, in which the government's intervention in their lives is to be limited, in which citizens feel that they are not "bad" but valued human beings, then we must teach the "bad" men this lesson. In the short run, defendants may find it easier to understand and deal with the system as it is, for it reflects a way of life they know well. But it does *not* reflect their aspirations of how they would like to live, and if they are to gain any hope of meeting their aspirations, it must.

———————————

1. John Griffiths, "Ideology in Criminal Procedure," *Yale Law Journal*, LXXIX (1970), 389–90. The quotation is from Robert Dreeben, "The Contribution of Schooling to the Learning of Norms," *Harvard Educational Review*, XXXVII (1967), 213–14.

INDEX